CHINESE COOKERY SECRETS

To eat a Chinese meal is to enjoy one of the truly delicious pleasures of life. The Chinese are artists when it comes to presentation, seasoning and combining, and their greatest skill is in choosing the freshest and most wholesome foods, and making the most of them. *Chinese Cookery Secrets* reveals exactly how the magic is accomplished. Written over fifty yeas ago, this is an authentic book on Chinese home cooking that is both a practical cookery book and a work of culinary history and culture that explains Chinese food preferences and describes the entire culinary process, beginning with the selection of ingredients and the best way to shop for them, preparation, Chinese utensils, the merits of different cooking methods, seasoning and menu composition before proceeding to the recipes themselves which are classified in fifteen different categories, displaying the variety of Chinese edible delights. These include recipes for meat, poultry, game, sea food, fish, noodles, vegetables and sweet-sour dishes as well as special sections on chafing dish and sandy pot cookery. The directions are unusually thorough, and Chan includes social and historical information relating to Chinese food and cooking throughout the text, which is lavishly illustrated with line drawings of ingredients to aid identification when shopping. The variety of dishes, background knowledge and detailed instructions from start to finish introduce the reader to a golden age of Chinese home cookery.

CHINESE COOKERY SECRETS

ESTHER CHAN

LONDON AND NEW YORK

First published 2005 by Kegan Paul

Published 2013 by Routledge
2 Park Square, Milton Park, Abingdon, Oxfordshire OX14 4RN
711 Third Avenue, New York, NY 10017, USA

First issued in paperback 2016

Routledge is an imprint of the Taylor & Francis Group, an informa business

© Kegan Paul, 2005

All rights reserved. No part of this book may be reprinted or reproduced or utilised in any form or by any electric, mechanical or other means, now known or hereafter invented, including photocopying or recording, or in any information storage or retrieval system, without permission in writing from the publishers.

British Library Cataloguing in Publication Data
Chan, Esther
Chinese cookery secrets. – (Library of culinary arts)
1.Cookery, Chinese
I.Title
641.5'951

ISBN 13: 978-1-138-97049-6 (pbk)
ISBN 13: 978-0-7103-1075-0 (hbk)

TABLE OF CONTENTS

Foreword by The Rt. Hon. Malcolm MacDonald
Preface by Lady Y. P. McNeice
Author's Note

Part I – GENERAL DIRECTIONS

	Page
Chapter 1 Cooking Utensils ...	1 — 2
„ 2 Choice and Variety of Food ...	4 — 6
„ 3 Seasoning ...	9 — 11
„ 4 Methods of Preparation ...	12 —
„ 5 Methods of Cooking ...	13 — 15
„ 6 Selection of Menu ...	16 — 17

Part II – RECIPES

Chapter 1 Chicken ...	18 — 29
„ 2 Duck ...	31 — 35
„ 3 Fish ...	38 — 44
„ 4 Meat ...	46 — 72
Pork ... Page 46 — 61	
Beef ... 61 — 68	
Mutton & Lamb ... 69 — 72	
„ 5 Game ...	73 — 75
„ 6 Sea Food ...	76 — 86
„ 7 Egg ...	87 — 91
„ 8 Vegetable ...	92 — 100
„ 9 Soup ...	103 — 116
Chafing Dish ... Page 112 — 115	
Sandy Pot ... — 116	
„ 10 Rice ...	117 — 122
„ 11 Noodles ...	123 — 127
„ 12 Pastry and Sweet Dishes ...	128 — 138
„ 13 Specialities ...	139 — 160
Sweet and Sour Dishes ... Page 139 — 148	
Bird's Nest ... 149 — 150	
Shark's Fins ... 151 — 152	
Chop Suey ... 155 — 156	
Seasonings ... 157 — 160	

Foreword

I know nothing about cooking Chinese food, but have considerable experience of consuming it.

To eat a Chinese dinner is to enjoy one of the truly delicious pleasures of life. Were I a skilled man-of-letters, I would write a volume about such a meal, and at every line of every page the reader's mouth would water. I would describe in detail the odd recipes and astonishing ingredients, the singular meats and unprecedented sauces, the mysterious appearance and seductive flavour of each dish. But the words at my command are too poor and the phrases too trite to essay more than this brief foreword to Mrs. Esther Chan's book.

One of the charming qualities of the Chinese is their delight in entertaining friends to almost interminable repasts. I have been a guest at scores of such feasts in private homes, public restaurants and even sacred temples. Often the courses number between half-a dozen and a dozen; but sometimes they greatly exceed that number. The most lavish entertainment which I ever attended included twenty-four courses and continued for several hours. It was merely the dinner of a small local Chinese Chamber of Commerce in a remote corner of Borneo, and was a modest, brief affair compared with the classic, Gargantuan banquets in some more fashionable places.

The Chinese are, above all, artists; and they display their noble creative gift as truly in the cooking of food as in carving jade, casting bronze, shaping procelain, fashioning calligraphy and painting pictures. Each dish is a triumph of the chef's skill, taste and imagination. He can conjure from the most unpromising materials dainty morsels of unbelievable exquisiteness. Who would have thought that such lowly, vulgar stuffs as sea-slug, birds' nests, bamboo-chips and sharks' fins could be presented in a manner to make discriminating gourmets well-nigh swoon with delight? The transformation is miraculous, and each successive item in a cook's repertoire seems to be more bold and magical than the last.

In my unsophisticated childhood I sometimes took umbrage at a nursery rhyme which ran:

> "What are little boys made of?
> Slugs and snails and puppy dogs' tails—
> That's what little boys are made of.
> What are little girls made of?
> Sugar and spice and all that's nice—
> That's what little girls are made of."

Since dining and wining with my Chinese friends in Malaya and Borneo I have lost my sense of grievance against the author of the jingle. I understand now that I should not have taken offence at its apparently insulting innuendo, for its seeming slur on the constitution of little boys is in fact a high tribute. Of slugs and snails the Chinese contrive dishes fit for Emperors to eat, and I have no doubt that of puppy dogs' tails they can concoct a feast worthy of the Gods.

How that necromancy is performed has often baffled me. Now Mrs. Chan has written a book to reveal some of its secrets, and to recite the ingredients which are hurled into the magicians's cauldron. I commend "Chinese Cookery Secrets" to all those who are capable of appreciating the good things of life.

Malcolm MacDonald
Commissioner General of South-East Asia

Preface

Mrs. Esther Chan has had long years of experience in cooking and in this book has gathered recipes from the different provinces of China. For those who have not been initiated into the mysteries of Oriental cooking, there will be fascination and wonder at the amazing variety of dishes, and to those who already appreciate the subtle flavour of Chinese food, this book will fulfil a long felt need.

The Chinese live to eat and they have left no stone unturned in the field of culinary art in their exploration into and their experiments with the gifts of nature.

Instead, enthusiasm and the cultivation of a taste for good food are the making of a good cook. Mrs. Chan has provided the knowledge. The rest is left to the reader.

Author's Note

This Book was started at the request of my friends while I was in the employment of the United States Military Advisory Group in Nanking, China, where I had a Chinese cooking class. Due to the unsettled political conditions I was forced to leave Nanking and I was unable to finish the book.

A few of my recipes were published by the Straits Times, after I came over to Singapore, and there were quite a few letters received from readers who requested to publish more recipes.

One of such letters published in the Straits Times reads as follows:

The Straits Times,

Saturday, March 17th, 1951.

THE RECIPES OF ASIA

I feel I must write and thank you for your articles on "Asian Recipes." The one I read on Sweet-Sour Dishes is one which I have been trying to see for years.

After reading it I immediately made a dish from the recipe which was very much appreciated by the family. Thank you, Mrs. Esther Chan.

I do hope that we shall have many more recipes published on the great variety of Eastern dishes.

Appreciative English Woman.

IPOH

To express my appreciation to my Western friends who lived in China before and those who live in Singapore I finally compiled this book.

To Mrs. Y. P. McNeice, I owe a debt of gratitude for her generous assistance in my work and Mr. and Mrs. K. Y. Chan for their constant encouragement.

ESTHER CHAN.

CHINESE COOKERY SECRETS

Some Press Opinions

"Mrs Chan, whose Asian Recipes will be familiar to Straits Times readers, has done a remarkable job of presentation, selection and Westernization. Not only has she classified her recipes in 15 distinct categories, but she has told us a good deal that Western amateurs should know if their ignorance is not to outstrip their appreciation; and she has given us a lecture on Chinese cooking utensils and ingredients simply but clearly illustrated."

The Straits Times,

10th November, 1952.

"This attractively illustrated and bound book discloses a wealth of secrets to the lover of Chinese food. Divided into two sections:—

Best features are illustrated guides to the Various Chinese Seasoning and Vegetables and Fish that are peculiar to this race of epicurians.

For non-Malayans who enjoy and relish Chinese food, but are faced with the problem of preparing these very same dishes in their own kitchens, this book will be found invaluable."

Singapore Standard

23rd November, 1952

中國烹飪秘訣

The Old Type of Chinese Kitchen

The New Type of Chinese Kitchen

The Western Type of Chinese Kitchen

Part I. General Directions

Chapter 1. Cooking Utensils

A typical old Chinese kitchen will not be able to boast of an array of bright, glistening enamel ware, latest model electric stove or gas stove with automatic signals, shut-offs, turn-ons and instrument board, refrigerator, egg beater, dish washer, electric kettle, coffee percolator and all the paraphernalia of this modern age.

Back in the olden days the Chinese had mud stoves with two or three cauldrons and wooden lids to cook meals for ten or twenty people in a family. Tin cans, hibachi (a kind of mud charcoal stove) were also used to cook an entire meal without tears, Copper ladles, iron frying shovels, gourds and calabashes were used to hold water or food stuffs. Rice was cooked in a brass pot, fish fried in an iron pan with a broken handle, mutton stewed properly in a vessel made from an empty petrol can, and tea prepared in a pot with a broken spout. Bottles were substitutes for rolling pins and chopsticks were egg beaters. The cleaver was used in chopping meat and as a mincer. Dishes were washed with a whiskbroom.

Despite all the primitive utensils used and limited facilities employed, China has a long history in culinary art.

Nowadays, in modern Chinese homes, some of the utensils employed for cooking are almost the same as in any Western home, but many are still bereft of modern cooking equipment. A good supply of pots and pans of various sizes is always necessary. For instance, pots used for slow-cooking such as braising, stewing and making soups must be heavy and thick; thin pans are to be used for various forms of frying. Deep-frying, of course, needs something deep enough in which to float the pieces to be deep-fried.

A Chinese family kitchen can get along fine without an oven, but it can never go without a good steamer of Chinese fashion. For ordinary steaming, there is no special equipment needed. All that is required is a saucepan big enough to hold a bowl. In the saucepan place 3 inches of water. Do not allow it to boil dry; a little water should be added from time to time during the process of steaming. If too much water is used the bowl will float, causing the ingredients in the bowl to pour out; if there is too little the temperature will be too low and a longer time for steaming is required. When pastry is steamed, a double boiler will not be able to serve the purpose because the steam does not get at the food; in that case perforated upper layer has to be used.

Cooking Utensils

In ordinary practice, rush leaves, pine needles, or a piece of clean white cloth are placed on a perforated layer to prevent sticking. In case a good steamer of Chinese fashion cannot be obtained in the market, a tin can be used. Pierce holes in the bottom and then place it in a bigger boiler. Chopsticks are very useful for both eating and cooking purposes. They are not only used to pick up things from the vessel or putting things into it; but they can be used as an egg beater.

Ladles, perforated ladles and frying slice shovels are used to handle food that is being cooked. The cleaver is used for cutting, chopping and even scaling nowadays. A cutting board, round in shape, which is made from the trunk of a tree always works hand-in-hand with the cleaver.

An oil strainer is used to drain off the oil for deep-frying. It is made from wire strings with a bamboo handle. A special kind of wooden rice steamer with a movable bamboo bottom is used to steamed rice in the South-west Provinces of China. For smoking, a certain kind of frame is used. The chafing dish and sandy-pot are served on the table.

Other kitchen accessories such as frying pan, kneeding board, rolling pin and aluminium pots of various sizes in a modern Chinese family kitchen are much the same as in a Western family.

Choice and Variety of Food

Chapter 2. Choice and Variety of Food

As regards foodstuffs, it would be well perhaps if once first alters some of the preconceived notions regarding the Chinese diet. Stories are told of Chinese people being mouse-eaters. Such ideas are fallacious though it is true that snakes are eaten in South China and dogs are eaten by some people. They do not in any case occupy a place in the menu.

The fundamental difference between Chinese and Western food lies in the method of cooking, not in the materials. There are two Chinese proverbs saying 'Feed moderately on wholesome food; garden herbs surpass rich viands,' and 'Only eat fresh fish and ripened rice.' From these two proverbs we understand that a delicious dish is not estimated by its cost but by the selection of the best types of foodstuffs and the choice of the right material for each particular dish.

In China, from the same chicken two or there dishes can be cooked—the breast for frying, legs for stewing or braising, back and head for boiling soup and liver and gizzard for frying. The exception is when a whole chicken in to be served on the table. Often Chinese chefs have a whole chicken braised or boiled for soup. But remember a young chicken is good for braising and frying; the hen is good for boiling soup.

Ducks are regarded as the second best fowl and geese the third. Games such as wild ducks and pheasants are not very often found in the market, though they are good for braising and frying.

In china, as in any other country, hen's eggs are used as food. Duck's eggs are not commonly used, but are good for making soup. Goose eggs are very seldom eaten. Pigeon's eggs are served quite often at feasts but seldom in home cooking.

In the Chinese sense, meat means pork, unless some other kind of meat is specified. This is because the Chinese regard pork as the popular meat. Different dishes will need different kinds of cuts. The advice of butchers and one's own common sense will solve half the problem of what to select for a certain dish. For instance, the lean part can be fried while the fat part can be stewed or braised. Legs are good when stewed or braised and pork bones and ribs are used for making soups. A good piece of rib with plenty of meat is sometimes used for braising or in making the popular sweet and sour dishes.

Choice and Variety of Food

The byes are usually more expensive than simple lean meat. Liver was considered a good thing in China long before scientists discovered its nutritive value. Kidneys, lungs, intestine and tripe are good when they are cleaned and cooked properly. This arrangement of materials, besides producing the most satisfactory result, provides for more variety.

Most of the fish eaten in China are fresh-water fish, except in cities along the coast where sea-fish abounds. Actually fresh-water fish is better than that taken from the sea, although it must at once be admitted that shark's fins are the exception. Ordinarily, these are not used much in home cooking. Fishes in China, are so plentiful and varied that they cannot all be mentioned by name. Carp, ell, bass, scup, mullet are good for braising; bream and perch are good for both steaming and braising. Shell fish are just as good.

Lobsters, prawns, and shrimps all belong to one family. Small river shrimps are best and they are widespread in China. In the crab class, the fresh-water crabs are best of all. When shelled they make a very good accompaniment to dishes, especially that of sharks's fins. The best way to eat crabs is to steam them and dip them in a sauce of ginger mixed with vinegar.

Fresh vegetables are numerous. There is no need to mention those which are unobtainable. However, there are Chinese vegetables common to those in foreign countries, these being the cucumber, spinach, radish, cauliflower, turnip, french beans, and carrots. Bean sprouts, pea sprouts and winter melon are found almost daily in the Chinese diet. Potatoes and sweet potatoes are not eaten as vegetables. There are two kinds of bamboo shoots in the market, the winter and spring bamboo. The former is more tasty and the price is more expensive.

The Chinese are great vegetables eaters. especially the poorer class. Cabbage and bean curd are regarded as a poor family's food. Soy beans are rich not only in starch but are also a most important source of protein and since most people cannot afford to eat much meat, bean and bean products are the most typical kind of economical food.

Many people think that Chinese live entirely on rice. The idea is a mistaken one and should be corrected. Rice does form a staple food in the diet of approximately two-fifths of the Chinese people but the majority

Choice and Variety of Food

of the population live upon wheat, barley and millet. Rice and millet are usually boiled or ground into flour to make into bread, noodles, etc.

There are in China stores specializing in preserved food such as shark's fins, "hundred-year-old" eggs and Chinese ham. The commonest preserved eatables are black fungus, dried mushrooms, bamboo shoots, dried transparent pea-starch noodles (vermicelli,) dried lilies, dried shrimps, salted vegetables and salted fish of various kinds.

In conclusion, the average Chinese thrives mainly on vegetables, eggs, bean products and meat. Fowls are less eaten, comparatively, yet the Chinese are able to maintain good health because they know how to make vegetables as palatable as meat and to utilize the value of vegetables to the fullest extent.

Arrow Roots

Dried Lilies

Water Chestnuts

Bean Curd

Mushrooms

Dried Strimps

White Nuts

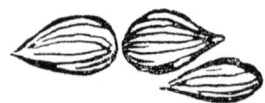
Almond

Star Aniseed

Lotus Seeds

Winter Bamboo Shoots

Spring Bamboo Shoot

White Fungus

Scallops

Bird's Nest

Sea-Slug

Shark's Fins (with Outer Skin)

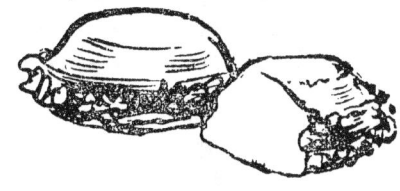
Shark's Fins (without Outer Skin)

Abalone

Dried Squids

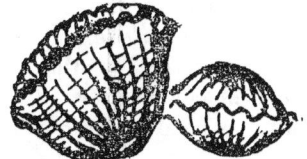
Clams

Razor Clams

Chapter 3. Seasoning

The chief aim of seasoning is to develop the original taste of food and to get rid of undesirable taste or odour. In Chinese cooking, wine is used very often because it takes away the strong, undesirable flavour that is found in fowl, duck, fish, shrimp, kidney and liver. Rice wine and yellow wine are good substitutes for dry sherry. Both rice and yellow wines are made from glutinous rice but yellow wine is to be preferred for cooking purposes. Never use distilled liquor for cooking, as it will spoil the taste.

Vinegar is also made from rice. It is indispensable in cooking fish, crabs, shrimps, etc. It is also served on the table. The best vinegar is the Chingkiang vinegar which is black in colour.

Fresh ginger and spring onion are absolutely necessary in the cooking of fish, chicken, liver, etc., to neutralize their strong flavours. Ginger used in cooking must be peeled and slices very thinly or chopped very fine as desired. In cooking fish, shrimps and crabs, ginger and spring onions are always used together. Spring onions sometimes are eaten raw when chopped and put on the top of a dish. The northerners in China are very fond of eating them raw.

In China, salt used for cooking is not so fine as the salt used in Western countries and it is more salty. Chinese dishes are know as "red-cooked" or "white-cooked" according to whether they are cooked with or without soy sauce. Soy sauce adds considerable salt to a dish, and allowance must be made for this when it is used for cooking. Generally speaking the sauce is only essential in braising or when it is needed for colour, though it is usual to dip "white-cooked" dishes in soy sauce when they are eaten. Soy sauce is made by soaking fermented soy beans in flour and salted water for a month or longer. The colour and consistency of sauce depend on the length of soaking. If Bovril or Oxo is used as a substitute, it fails to give the distinctive soy flavour, although it provides the colour.

There are several kinds of soy sauce in the market. The dark thick sauce with a strong colour but comparatively mild in flavour is called *"chu-yan"* in Cantonese. It is widely used in restaurants. Another light-coloured variety, without enough colour for use in cookery, but with fine flavour, is called *"chan-ch'an."* The most suitable sauce for general use is called *"chan-yan"* in Mandarin. (Similar to soy sauce is Soy Jam which is thicker in consistency and also used in cooking.) Oyster sauce is expensive and it is used sometimes but less often than soy sauce in family cooking.

Seasoning

Sugar is used mostly when making refreshments, and rock sugar is especially good for his purpose. For frying and braising dishes a little sugar is often used to sweeten the dish.

Starch is commonly used to thicken cooking and may be obtained from pea-flour, water caltrops or flour water residue. Cornstarch and cornflour may be used as substitutes. Wheat flour is used as a heavier binder. Pieces of meat or fish are often dipped in a paste of flour mixed with beaten eggs in deep-frying.

Szechuan pepper in the form of ungrounded seeds is used very often in China. It is a very ingratiating spice which tastes only faintly hot but brings out the taste of many foodstuffs very well. Star aniseed or powder is similar but the smell is slightly different. Cinnamon may be served as a good substitute for both. The Chinese parsley is tender and rich in flavour. It is often used for garnishing, but the warmth of the cooked food also brings out its best flavour. Some people have to learn to like it.

As for cooking oil, peanut oil, bean oil, vegetable oil and lard are used according to the nature of the dish. Some people do not like the smell of vegetable oil or bean oil. Peanut oil is preferred for deep-frying. Never use lard for deep-frying because the food in which it is fried turns out soft and not crisp.

Vegetables taste best when fried in lard. Foods cooked in vegetable oil can be eaten cold but those cooked in lard are good only the first time or when warmed up because during cold days it freezes very easily. Crisco or other cooking fat is not desirable for use in Chinese cooking because it could not be right. For the recipes in this book both lard and peanut oil or cooking oil can be used except that lard is preferable for frying dishes and vegetable oil is best for deep-frying.

Lard made from fresh pork fat is better than that in tins sold in markets. Cut the pork fat into pieces and put about ½ cup of water for 1 lb. lard in a frying pan and heat on a moderate fire. When the water evaporates the fat begins to melt. Pour into a heat-resisting container or a bowl and allow it to cool. Place it in the refrigerator or in any other cool place. Scoop as needed.

Sesame oil is used in small quantities because it is too expensive for cooking. Vegetarians in China use it very liberally. If sesame seeds are available in the market it is easy to make the oil at home and it is less expensive. Olive oil can be used as a substitute.

Seasoning

Duck fat and chicken fat are used and are good for cooking. Chinese Muslims are great users of duck fat in China. In Nanking the salt-water duck shops are usually run by Chinese Muslims.

It is quite popular in China to use glutomate or flavouring powder to enhance the taste of a dish. The disadvantage is that it affects the palate as it makes all dishes taste alike. An expert cook need never depend on this powder. Food in a restaurant is delicious but no one would like to eat it every day because the flavouring powder is used too liberally.

Methods of Preparation

Chapter 4.   Methods of Preparation

With regard to the method of preparation, Chinese chefs and housewives generally cut up the meat and vegetable before cooking while in Western countries the diner generally does the cutting. This is one of the reasons why chopsticks are used by the Chinese while Westerners still cannot dispense with knives and forks.

Cutting is important because it determines the appearance of the dish and length of time required for cooking. There are various forms of cutting, such as large squares for braising and stewing, thin slices and fine strips for frying. In the case of mixed dishes, the choice of the method of cutting is usually determined by the nature of vegetables or dried vegetables, such as dried mushrooms, dried fungus, dried shrimps, etc., or by the appearance of the accompanying dishes. For instance, if four dishes are served on the table it is better to have one dish cut in squares, one in slices, one in dices and one in shreds for soup. In general, dices are suitable for peas and beans; strips for bamboo shoots and slices for mushrooms. However, there is no hard and fast rule and individual taste should prevail.

There is a typical method of cutting cylindrical shaped vegetables like carrots, asparagus, turnips and cucumbers. First cut an angle from the axis; then roll the cylindrical vegetable slightly and cut it further up so that the new cut will partly cut across the original cut surface and partly cut a new surface. However, they are sometimes cut into slices or other forms depending on individual recipes.

Preserved food such as mushrooms, dried shrimps, scallops and fungus should be washed first and then soaked in water or wine. The quantity of water or wine to be used is flexible, but remember to save the water or wine in which the ingredients are soaked, for further cooking.

Chapter 5. Methods of Cooking

Special methods are used for different recipes. They are only mentioned in a general way.

With regard to the method of cooking, it should be mentioned that there are more than 100 different Chinese characters or words denoting cooking. Thus, *Hsia, Cha, Chien, Chao,* etc., translated into English mean "to fry." The shades of difference are so obscure that they baffle description, and any attempt to be too precise could only result in confusion.

To simplify or to make the recipes more practical, Chinese methods of cooking can roughly be classified into the following main categories: —

1. Pure-Stewing. It differs from braising in several ways. Firstly, no soy sauce is used; so its sauce is clear. Secondly, it is less dry, for such method requires slow cooking which yields clear soup. A low fire should be used as soon as boiling starts. Ordinary pure stewing materials are : pork leg, pork shoulder, pork sides with skin, whole duck, whole chicken, fish head and whole or half piece of shad. The advantage of pure-stewing is that it contains part of a main dish and part of soup, and it brings out the good eating qualities and shows up the poor eating grades. Pot-stewing belongs to this class, the only difference is that the pot in which the condiments are stewed is served on the table instead of pouring it out into another bowl to serve.

2. Braising. In the Chinese sense, this is stewing with soy sauce Before braising the meat in soy sauce, pre-frying is required in some cases. Braising takes a long time to cook, so it is a typical form of family cooking. Moreover, it cooks down a lot of foodstuffs so that it is not profitable for restaurant owners to adopt this method.

The advantage of braising food is that it can be kept for a few days and it tastes just as good after it has been warmed up again. Cold braised jelly meat, chicken, etc., are especially good; moreover, they can be "stretched to last" by adding vegetables such as spinach, celery, cabbage, etc. The usual way is to fry the vegetables first, then warm up the braised meat, etc., and add to the vegetables which becomes more tasty with the brown gravy. Ordinary meats used are: pork leg, pork shoulder, pork sides with skin, beef, mutton, lamb, leg of mutton with skin, whole chicken, whole duck, carp, mullet and bream.

Methods of Cooking

Pot-braising is a branch of this family. The only difference is that this kind of braising is on a very large scale, long-term operation and more spices are used. First boil the chicken or duck with skin and bone for an hour; then add spring onion, ginger, aniseed, Szechuan pepper, and a liberal amount of cooking wine and soy sauce. After cooking, take out the meat or fowl and save the gravy for future use. The original sauce is called the master sauce which should be strengthened with soy sauce, salt, wine and spices. Before putting away, the sauce should be sterilized by heating each time it has been touched by raw material or unsterilized ladles. Home made pot-braising is always a small process and the sauce need never be kept so long as is done in restaurants.

3. **Frying** Frying is the most practical method of cooking. Meats most suitable for trying are fillet or other parts of pork, beef, lamb, where there is no tendon but uniform meat. Tenderness is an important point and the meat must be cut across or against the grain. Vegetables should be used young. Hard vegetables such as cabbage, bean sprouts, cauliflower, french beans, turnips and carrots, etc., should be fried slightly and a small amount of water added to help them to cook in their own juice. Leaf vegetables such as spinach, celery, lettuce, etc., should be fried quickly as themselves contain sufficient water and no more is required than what is left on after washing.

While frying usually takes only two or three minutes, the preparation of materials involves a lot of time. All the fried dishes should be served as soon as done and eaten as soon as served. For these dishes a brisk fire is always the important element.

Deep-frying is another method which is a preparatory process and a complete dish-making. The commonest way of preparing meat which is to be deep-fried is to cut it into medium sized pieces. In the case of fish desired to be served whole, make a few slashes across it, soak in prepared seasoning for a while and fry in hot deep fat. A coating of starch or egg-flour is sometimes used in deep-frying.

Opposite to deep-frying is shallow frying, which does not need so much oil. Pastry is sometimes shallow-fried, especially after it is first boiled.

4. **Roasting.** Without ovens, roasting is done over a charcoal fire by turning the roast slowly round and round. There is not much roasting done at home, for roasting in China is always done in restaurants,

therefore, roasting is not a family method of cooking in China. Cantonese restaurants excel especially in this line. Chicken, duck, goose are quite commonly roasted whole. Peiping restaurants are famous for roast ducks. The Chinese way of roasting is similar to that of the West, except that the Chinese sometimes smear soy sauce, sesame oil or lard on the skin so that it is kept brown, shiny and juicy. Since most of our Western friends have the facilities for roasting, I shall mention some suitable recipes.

5. Steaming. Steaming preserves all the nutritive elements and the food can never be burned if water is added to the saucepan from time to time. (First, fill the steamer pot with water; into this place the steamed bowl. Occasionally add water if it appears to be dried up.) The length of steaming time varies according to the nature of the dish. Sometimes the cooking materials are mixed first and sometimes no water need be added to the steamed bowl in the presence of natural juice and condensed steam. (Crabs are perferably steamed rather than actually boiled.)

6. Smoking. In China, the smoking of fish, poultry, egg and meat is not uncommon. Saw dust and aniseed powder are used for smoking. Brown sugar is a good substitute for saw dust.

In conclusion, since Chinese cooking needs a good range of heat, gas stoves are preferable to electric stoves.

Selection of Menu

Chapter 6. Selection of Menu

This book contains three hundred recipes which are divided into different groups: namely, chicken, duck, fish, etc. Except where mention is made of a whole duck, whole chicken, 3 lbs. or 4 lbs. braised leg of pork etc., each recipe should be ample for four people. The Chinese menu usually consists of four dishes and a soup for a meal for four people, five dishes and one soup for five and so on.

A typical Chinese family meal consists of four dishes including a vegetable dish and a soup. A six dish menu, two vegetable dishes may be chosen but there should be only one soup, though the soup bowl may be refilled according to requirements.

The following are suggested menus for some meals taken from recipes of this book:—

Menu I   (*For two persons*)

Fried Diced Chicken with Walnuts
Fried Spinach
Mushrooms Soup
Plain Rice or Fried Egg and Rice

Menu II   (*For three persons*)

Sweet and Sour Fish
Fried Fresh Peas
Fried Beef with Green Pepper
Cabbage and Bean Curd Soup
Plain Rice or Fried Noodles

Menu III   (*For four persons*)

Prawn *Fu-Yung*
Fried Liver
Braised Pork Chop
Sweet and Sour Cabbage
Chicken Shreds and Mushrooms Soup
Plain Rice or Steamed Fancy Rolls

Selection of Menu

Menu IV *(For five persons)*

Fried Pork Shreds with Pea Sprouts
Paper-Wrapped Chicken
Steamed Whole Fish
Sweet and Sour Pork
Creamed Cabbage
Pig's Liver Soup
Plain Rice or Steamed Bread (*Man-T'ou*)

Menu V *(For six persons)*

Fried Stuffed-Duck with Glutinous Rice
Fried Tomato Beef
Braised Mutton or Lamb
Scrambled Eggs with Shrimps
Fried Lettuce
Dried Shrimps with Spinach
Potato and Pork-Bone Soup
Plain Rice or White Congee

Menu VI *(For seven persons)*

Fried Fish with Mushrooms
White Jellied Chicken
Fried Kidney with Cauliflower
Fried Lamb with Young Leeks
Sweet and Sour Cabbage
Creamed Bamboo Shoots
Meat Ball and Chinese Vermicelli Soup
Plain Rice or Fried Crispy Noodles

Menu VII *(For eight persons)*

Chicken Fillet with Omelet
Braised Pork with Cabbage
Fried Prawns with Green Peas
Steamed Ham and Eggs
Fried Squids
Fried Winter Melon
Fried Celery with Pea Sprout
Fish Head and Turnip Soup
Plain Rice or Assorted Fried Rice

Chicken

Part II. Recipes

雞
Chapter 1. Chicken

In China, as is in other countries, chicken has preference over other kinds of meat. (As in a Western dinner party, when chicken is made the main dish, a few fowls must be killed.) It is very convenient at a Chinese party that the same chicken can be prepared for several dishes if desired. For instance, the white meat can be sliced and fried. Dark meat and bones can be used for soup. The meat of the soup, if not overcooked, can be used for Chinese chicken salad, " white cut chicken " or cold jellied chiken. (In some cases, when the white meat is fried the black meat can be deep-fried or braised.) The liver and gizzard can be fried. (Wings, leg and feet are sold in the market and they are used in some popular dishes.)

It is also customary to use a whole chicken for soup making, deep frying or braising. In such cases, young chicken is preferred for frying, braising or steaming. Old hens are always used for boiling soup. (Unless specified, chicken in China means either old and young fowls in a general sense.) Old roosters are rarely eaten. Chinese consider the meat of a young roosters to be highly nutritious until it starts crowing; thereafter it is believed to have injurious properties. (If the chicken is an old fowl always use its own fat to fry the chicken meat before braising otherwise use 4 tablespoonfuls of cooking oil as substitute.) A longer time is needed to braise an old fowl.

紅　燒　雞
Braised Chicken

1 young chicken
4 tb-sp cooking oil
½ t-sp sugar
½ cup soy sauce

2 tb-sp sherry (optional)
3—4 slices fresh ginger
1 spring onion

Singe and wash the chicken and cut into 1½ inch square pieces without separating the bones.

Heat the cooking oil in a heavy pot till hot, put the chicken in and stir for 2 or 3 minutes. Then add 2 cups of water, soy sauce, ginger and spring onion.

Turn fire low after it comes to boil and simmer for ½ hour or 1 hour keeping the saucepan tightly covered. Add sugar and cook for another 10 minutes.

Chicken

(If the fowl is an old chicken, a little more water should be added and a longer time is needed.)

紅 燒 冬 菰 雞 塊
Braised Chicken With Mushrooms

1 fat spring chicken
20 mushrooms (big)
2 oz. ham
¼ cup soy sauce
4 tb-sp cooking oil
½ cup sherry (optional)
1 spring onion
3—4 slices ginger
1 t-sp salt

Clean and wash the chicken thoroughly and cut into pieces. Heat the cooking oil and fry the chicken as in the preceding recipe. Add 2½ cups of water. Heat quickly until it comes to the boil and cover the pot tightly. Cook on a medium fire for 30 minutes. Add salt, minced ham, soy sauce, mushroom and spring onion. (Remove the stems from the mushroom and wash.) Simmer for another 20 minutes or longer before serving.

The chicken should be served in a deep bowl or a soup plate with the gravy it is cooked in.

紅 燒 粟 子 雞
Braised Chicken With Chestnuts

1 young chicken
1 lb. chestnuts
6 tb-sp cooking oil
½ cup soy sauce
3—4 slices ginger
1 spring onion
½ tb-sp salt

Clean and wash the chicken and cut into 1 inch square pieces without removing the bones. Heat the cooking oil in a heavy pot, add the chicken and keep on stirring for a minute or two. Add soy sauce and stir for another minute, then pour in 2 cups of water. Cover the pot tightly and heat over a big fire until boiling.

Cut the spring onion into small sections about 1 inch in length and put it into the pot with the ginger. Turn to a low fire and cook for 20 minutes.

Soak the chestnuts in hot water for 10 minutes. Peel off the outside and inside skin, then add them into the pot and 1 more cup of water. Add ½ t-sp salt. Cover tight and simmer together with chicken over a low fire for another ½ hour.

Chicken

凍 雞
White Jellied Chicken

1 young chicken
½ tb-sp salt

1 tb-sp sherry (optional)
A few spring onions

Choose a young bird. Singe and clean properly. Boil 1½ pints of water in a big sauce-pan with ½ tb-sp salt, sherry and spring onions. Drop the chicken in, when the water is boiling; and cook on a low fire for 1 hour. Remove the sauce-pan from the fire and leave the chicken in the soup for 4 hours. When the chicken is cold and firm, cut the breast into two, then remove wings and legs, and separate the bone. Cut the meat into squares and arrange the pieces in a bowl.

Stew the bones separately with the original soup for ½ hour over a low fire; pour the soup over the cut chicken into the bowl and leave it in a refrigerator over-night. Turn the contents out on to a plate and decorate with parsley if desired.

紙 包 雞
Paper-Wrapped Chicken

2 young chickens
1 cup green peas,
Few slices ham
2 tb-sp soy sauce
1 spring onion
2—3 slices ginger
1 t-sp salt

1 lb. vegetable oil
20 pieces cellophane paper or grease paper
1 tb-sp sherry (optional)
½ t-sp sugar
½ t-sp pepper

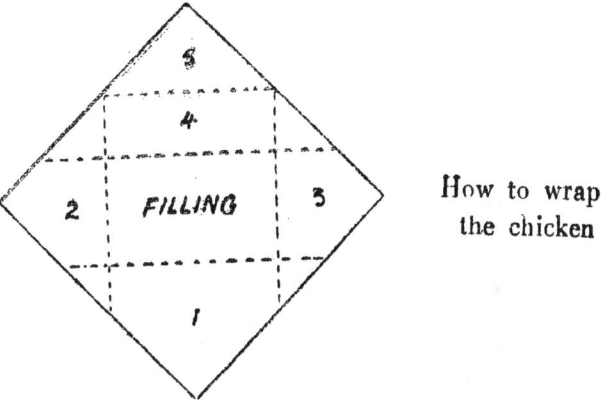

How to wrap the chicken

Chicken

Remove the bones and skin of the chicken and cut into slices, about 1/8 inch thick, by 1/2 inch wide, by 1 1/2 inches long. Put soy sauce, sherry, chopped spring onions, chopped ginger, salt and sugar in a bowl and soak the sliced chicken, ham and green peas in the mixture for 20 minutes. Then divide the chicken into 20 portions and cut the cellophane 4 by 4 inches; then fold each portions in a piece of cellophane paper. Spread a little lard on each piece of paper before wrapping.

Heat the cooking oil and fry the packages for 2 minutes. Serve hot and without unwrapping the paper so that the juice and heat can be kept. If the frying pan is too small to fry them in one lot; then fry them in four or five lots. After finishing the first lot, heat the oil until boiling, before frying the next.

西 瓜 雞
Water-Melon Chicken

1 young chicken	2 tb-sp sherry (optional)
1 water melon (small)	1 tb-sp salt

Clean the chicken and place it in a heavy pot with salt, sherry and two bowls of water, and boil over a low for 1/2 hour.

Remove the top of the water-melon and scoop out enough of the melon to enable the chicken to be placed in it. Pour in the chicken and the gravy and use the top of the melon to cover it. Place it in a pot, big enough to hold the whole melon and steam for 1 1/2 hour continuously under a low fire. Add a little water into the pot occasionally if necessary. When the skin of the melon becomes yellow it is ready to serve. Both the chicken and the meat of the melon are delicious. Place the whole melon into a big bowl and serve.

叫 化 雞
Beggar's Chicken

1 chicken	1 tb-sp salt
2 tb-sp sherry (optional)	1 spring onion
2 tb-soy sauce	2 slices ginger
mud (enough to make a coating)	1 t-sp aniseed powder

Kill the chicken but do not remove the feathers. Cut about 1 1/2 inches long at the back of the tail and remove everything inside the chicken. Use a piece of wet clean cloth to wipe off the blood then rinse it; do this a few times. Rub thoroughly with salt and put in the soy sauce, sherry, spring onions, ginger and aniseed powder. Then stitch it up so that the contents will not spill out.

Chicken

Mix the mud with water and coat the chicken, then put it in the fire and turn it around several times. As soon as the fragrance of the chicken can be smelled and when the mud is entirely dried up the chicken is cooked. Remove the mud and feathers, cut chicken into pieces and serve.

This recipe is famous in Chekiang Province and it is so called possibly because it is not cooked in a proper kitchen and any beggar can cook it.

清 蒸 鳳 爪
Steamed Chicken Wings and Legs

10 wings	1 tb-sp soy sauce
10 legs	1 t-sp cornflour
½ t-sp salt	¼ lb. mushrooms

Chop the wings into two and throw away the lowest part. Cut of the claws of the legs and leave them in whole pieces. Mix them with soy sauce and cornflour. Soak the mushrooms in hot water and cut off the stems. Put the wings and legs and mushrooms in a deep basin or bowl and steam in a steamer or boiler at a moderate heat for 1 hour. Test with a fork, cook a little longer if necessary. The length of time required for cooking depends on the size of the legs and wings. Serve with pepper.

清 蒸 雞
Steamed Chicken

1 spring chicken	Few slices of ginger
2 t-sp salt	1 spring onion

Select a young bird. Singe and clean thoroughly. Put in a large basin with ½ pint of water, a few pieces of ginger, 1 spring onion and 2 t-sp salt. Place the basin in a large boiler or steamer and steam for 2 hours at a moderate heat after the water starts to boil. It is ready to serve when the chicken can be easily pierced with a fork or chopsticks.

燻 雞
Smoked Chicken

1 chicken	3/4 cup cooking oil
3/4 cup soy sauce	1 lb. saw dust
1 t-sp salt	1 t-sp aniseed powder or
10 spring onions	3 tb-sp brown sugar
1 tb-sp sherry	

Chicken

Singe and clean the chicken. Cut into halves. Put in a heavy boiler with 1½ cups of water and 3 spring onions and simmer on a low fire for ½ an hour after boiling. Add in sherry, ½ cup soy sauce and salt. Half and hour later remove from fire and put the cooked chicken on a perforated plate or an iron grate on a heavy iron pot. Grease the sawdust and aniseed powder or the brown sugar into the heavy pot and cover tightly and apply a big fire. Smoke on a big fire for 3 minutes; after the chicken is brown it is ready to serve. Heat the cooking oil and mix in the chopped spring onion and remaining soy sauce and pour on top of the smoked chicken and serve.

白 斬 雞

White-Cut Chicken

1 fat chicken
1 tb-sp salt
1 spring onion

2 tb-sp sesame oil or salad oil
1 slice of ginger
1 tb-sp sherry

Wash the chicken thoroughly. Boil 2 pints of water in a pot, add salt and sherry. Put the ginger and onion inside the chicken and place it in the boiling water and boil for another 5 minutes. If there is any chicken fat put it into the pot also. Remove the pot from the fire and cover tight and when the water is cold, rub the chicken with lard cut into pieces and serve with soy sauce and pepper if desired.

For this recipe it is preferable to use pigs trotter soup, instead of water. See recipe of Pigs Trotter Soup.

冷 拌 雞 絲

Chinese Chicken Salad

1 spring chicken
1 small bunch celery
1 tb-sp sesame or salad oil

1 tb-sp soy sauce
1 t-sp sugar
½ t-sp salt

Wash the chicken clean and put it in a heavy pot with 4 bowls of water. After the water boils, simmer on a low fire until the chicken is tender. Remove from fire and save the water in which the chicken is boiled for soup.

Cut the celery into long pieces and boil in a little water just to cover the celery for 1 minute. Drain and rinse the chiken and celery in cold water. Remove the bones and skin from the chiken and tear the chicken into inch long pieces. Tearing meat always tastes better because the meat gives a better surface to absorb the seasoning. Mix the celery, chicken meat, oil, soy sauce salt and sugar and serve.

Chicken

芙 蓉 雞 絲
Chicken Fillet With Omelet

1 spring chicken	Spring onion (few pieces)
4 eggs	1 t-sp salt
½ tb-sp sherry (optional)	4 tb-sp lard
Few slices ginger	1 tb-sp cornflour

Clean the chicken and cut only the white meat into shreds. Save the rest for making soup. Beat the eggs well and cut the onion into 1 inch sections. Add the chicken shreds into the beaten eggs and mix with 1 tb-sp water, sherry, cornflour and salt.

Heat the lard until smoking hot and put the chicken, sectioned spring onion and chopped ginger. Stir constantly on a good brisk fire for 2 minutes. Cook just before serving because the chicken gets tough if it is re-heated or kept in an oven.

什 錦 雞 丁
Assorted Chicken Dices

1 spring chicken	1 t-sp salt
2 ozs. mushroom	3 tb-sp soy sauce
¼ lb. water chestnuts	1 tb-sp sherry (optional)
¼ lb. winter bamboo shoots	½ lb. cooking oil
½ cup green peas	2—3 slices ginger
¼ lb. dry almonds and walnuts	1 tb-sp cornflour
	1 spring onion

Cut the white meat of the chicken into dices, mix with the cornflour, 1 tb-sp water, sherry, ½ t-sp salt, chopped spring onion and ginger. Soak the almonds and walnuts in hot water and peel off the inner skin, then chop them into dices. Heat the cooking oil till hot and fry the nuts for 1 minute until light brown. Take them out and save the oil for other purposes.

Soak the mushrooms in hot water then cut the mushrooms, water chestnuts and bamboo shoots after the size of the nuts. Fry the mushrooms, water chestnuts and bamboo shoots with 4 tb-sp oil and add ½ t-sp salt and stir for 2 minutes then remove from fire. Heat another 4 tb-sp oil and put the chicken in and fry over a big fire. Stir constantly for 2 minutes, then add in the mushrooms, water chestnuts, bamboo shoots and green peas. Add in the soy sauce and cook them for ½ minute together. Remove from fire. Mix in the fried almonds and walnuts and serve.

In case water chestnuts are not available just leave them out.

Chicken

蠔 油 雞 球
Fried Chicken Balls With Oyster Sauce

1 spring chicken
1 t-sp salt
1 tb-sp cornflour
1 tb-sp sherry (optional)
2—3 slices ginger

1 small onion
4 tb-sp lard
2 tb-sp oyster sauce
1 t-sp sugar

Remove the skin of the chicken and take off all the bones with a sharp cleaver or knife. Mince the meat and cut the spring onion and ginger into small sections. Mix the sherry, salt, cornflour and about 2 tb-sp of water with the chopped chicken meat and again mix them thoroughly. Use the palms to make them into small balls approximately about the size of pigeon eggs.

Heat the lard till hot, put the seasoned chicken balls in and fry them for about 5 minutes. Stir constantly while frying, then add in the oyster sauce, sugar, and onion shreds and chopped ginger. Cook and stir 5 minutes more. Add in ¼ cup of water while cooking if the gravy has a tendency to become too dry. Sprinkle with pepper when serving.

青 椒 炒 雞 塊
Fried Chicken With Green Pepper

1 spring chicken
6 large green peppers
¼ cup soy sauce
4 tb-sp lard

1 tb-sp sherry (optional)
1 t-sp salt
1 cup flour

Wash and clean the chicken thoroughly. Cut into pieces about 1 inch square and remove all the bones with a sharp cleaver.

Mix the flour with sufficient water to make a thick paste and dip the small pieces of chicken into it until well coated. Heat 3 tablespoonsful of lard and fry the pieces of chicken until a light brown. Then remove from the pan.

Take away all the seeds from the pepper and cut them about the same size as the chicken. Fry them in the pan with the last tablespoonful of lard. Replace the chicken, add the soy sauce, sherry, sugar and salt.

Chicken

If necessary a little water may be added to prevent the mixture from sticking.

韭菜黄炒雞片
Fried Chicken With Young Leeks

1 young chicken
1 tb-sp sherry (optional)
½ lb. young leeks
2—3 slices ginger

4 tb-sp lard or cooking oil
3 tb-sp soy sauce
1 t-sp salt

Cut the chicken into slices and use only white meat. Cut the leeks about 1½ inches in length. Heat 2 tb-sp lard and fry the leeks first for 1 minute. Add ½ t-sp salt and remove it from fire. Heat the remaining oil and put in the chicken and ginger. Stir constantly for 2 minutes and pour in the sherry, ½ t-sp salt and soy sauce.

Add the leeks and stir for 1 minute more. A good brisk fire is necessary throughout the whole process of cooking.

冬筍炒雞絲
Chicken Shreds With Bamboo Shoots

1 spring chicken
1 tb-sp cornflour
1 lb. winter bamboo shoots
1 tb-sp sherry (optional)

2 tb-soy sauce
6 tb-sp lard
1 spring onion
½ t-sp salt
2 slices ginger

Cut the chicken into shreds and use only the white meat. Mix the chopped spring onions, ginger, sherry, soy sauce, cornflour and 2 tb-sp water.

Shred the bamboo shoots and fry in half the fat which must be smoking. Add the salt, stir for 1 minute and remove from the fire. Heat the remaining fat and fry the chicken for 2 minutes. Pour in the bamboo shoots and soy sauce mixture and stir together over a good brisk fire 2 minutes more. Serve hot.

If desired, green pepper can be substituted for bamboo shoots. Remove the seeds of the pepper and follow the same methods of cooking.

Chicken

核 桃 炒 雞 丁
Fried Diced Chicken With Walnuts

½ chicken
6 big mushrooms
1 cup walnuts
2 tb-sp soy sauce

½ tb-sp cornflour
1 t-sp salt
½ t-sp sugar
1 lb. cooking oil

Shell and dice the walnuts. Heat the oil and fry the nuts until they are a golden brown. Remove from the fire and blot on heavy Manila paper.

Clean and dice the chicken and place about 4 tb-sp of oil in a frying pan, pouring in the diced chicken when the oil is smoking hot. Stir for 1 minute. Have the cornflour, sugar, salt, 2 lb-sp water and soy sauce thoroughly mixed together and pour the mixture on the top of the frying chicken.

Soak the mushrooms in hot water for about 10 minutes and dice them. Add them to the mixture in the frying pan and stir for 5 minutes until the mushrooms are tender. Remove from fire. Mix them with the deep-fried walnuts while serving.

冬 菰 炒 雞 片
Fried Chicken With Mushrooms

1 chicken breast
1 tb-sp cornflour
? tb-sp sherry (optional)
4 tb-sp lard

¼ lb. mushrooms
½ t-sp salt
1 tb-sp soy sauce

Take the chicken breast and cut into thin slices. Mix with sherry, soy sauce and cornflour. Soak the mushrooms in hot water as usual and fry with half of the lard and salt. Pour in the mushroom water and cook for 5 minutes then remove from the fire. Heat the other half of the fat till hot and drop the seasoned chicken in to fry for 3 minutes till every piece of chicken turns white. Keep stirring while frying. Mix in the mushrooms and serve.

冬 菰 炒 雞 雜
Fried Chicken Liver and Gizzard With Mushrooms

½ lb. chicken liver and gizzard

2 t-sp cornflour
1 tb-sp sherry (optional

Chicken

¼ lb. mushrooms
½ lb. bamboo shoots
1 onion
1 tb-sp soy sauce
½ t-sp salt
6 tb-sp lard

Wash the liver and gizzard, cut off the white skin of the gizzard. Cut the liver into slices and each gizzard into quarters and make a few slashes crosswise on the gizzards. Wash the mushrooms and soak them in hot water. Cut the bamboo shoots and throw away the tough parts and shred the onion.

Fry the onion shreds, mushroom and bamboo shoot slices in 2 tb-sp lard and ½ t-sp salt for 5 minutes. Put then on one side of the frying pan and heat the remaining lard. Mix the cornflour, sherry and soy sauce with the gizzard and liver. Fry them for 3 minutes then mix in the bamboo shoots, onion and mushroom. Serve hot.

炸 全 雞
Deep-Oil-Fried Chicken

1 young chicken
2 t-sp salt
1 tb-sp sherry (optional)
1 spring onion
1 lb. cooking oil

Singe and wash the chicken. Remove the entrails from the tail of the chicken. Rub the sherry on both the inside and outside of the chicken. Hang the chicken to dry for 1 hour before cooking. Put the spring onion and ginger inside the chicken.

Heat the cooking oil till hot and fry the chicken all over until golden brown. For a medium-sized chicken allow half an hour for frying and while frying baste the chicken constantly both inside and outside. Cut the chicken into pieces and season with pepper before serving.

炸 八 塊
Fried Spring Chicken

2 spring chickens
3 tb-sp soy sauce
1 lb. cooking oil
1 t-sp salt
½ t-sp sugar
1 spring onion
2 cups cornflour

Clean and wash the chicken thoroughly and chop each chicken into eight pieces, legs, wings, two pieces of the back and two pieces of the breast. Cut the spring onion into small pieces. Put them in a bowl with the chicken and add the soy sauce salt and sugar. Then let it stand for 1 hour. Dip each piece into the cornflour so that it is well covered with flour. Fry the pieces in hot oil till they are a golden brown. If the frying pan is too small to hold all the pieces together, fry them in two or three lots. Serve with pepper.

炸 雞 脯
Fried Chicken Breast

4 chicken breasts	4 tb-sp soy sauce
½ cup flour	4 tb-sp sherry (optional)
1 lb. cooking oil	½ t-sp sugar
½ t-sp salt	

Cut the chicken breasts into 1 inch squares without separating the bones. Mix the flour with ½ cup of water and ½ t-sp salt. Heat the cooking oil till smoking. Dip each piece of chicken into the flour until well coated. Fry the pieces in hot oil till golden brown. Drain well and put them in a bowl containing soy sauce, sherry and sugar. Mix well. Sprinkle with pepper and serve.

炸 雞 珍 肝
Deep Fried Chicken Gizzard

½ lb. gizzard	1 lb. cooking oil
1 cup cornflour	½ t-sp salt
1 tb-sp soy sauce	

Clean the gizzards and remove the white skin inside. Cut them into pieces and cut a few slashes crosswise on each piece. Mix them with soy sauce, salt, and cornflour. Heat the cooking oil until smoking and fry them for 5 minutes. Sprinkle with pepper and serve.

Duck's gizzard can be cooked in the same manner.

Duck in the Larder (before roasting)

Duck

鴨

Chapter 2. Duck

Duck is more commonly eaten in China than in any other country probably because of the variety of ways of preparing it. Duck is salted, roasted, braised, simmered, fried and soup-boiled. Nanking people are specialists in making salted water-duck and Peking people are experts in roasting duck. The Cantonese people are also clever in preparing the roast duck and salted-duck but the methods they employ are different from those of the Nanking and Peking people. Duck stored in vegetable oil and taken out to steam when needed is very popular in Canton.

In China special dishes are prepared on special festivals and different seasons. Duck is eaten more during the Moon-Festival—15th day of the Eight Month than at any other time of the year. Salted-duck is usually eaten in winter because then the duck is not so easily " spoiled."

Duck's gizzard and liver are eaten as much as those of the chicken. Duck's gizzard is usually salted and dried in the sun and then cooked and sliced. This makes a good accompanying dish with congee at breakfast. It is especially good when it is seasoned with a little sesame oil. Duck's feet, tongue, and liver are also great delicacies.

紅 燒 全 鴨

Whole Brown-Braised Duck

1 fat duck
8 tb-sp soy sauce
2 tb-sp sherry (optional)
1 slice ginger
2—3 spring onions
6 tb-sp lard or cooking oil
½ t-sp sugar

Clean the duck thoroughly and remove the oil sacs which smell very strongly, though some people like them. Make a cut about 1½ inches long at the back of the tail and draw the bird. Break the legs so that the duck can sit on the plate, instead of stretching out its legs, after being cooked.

Mix the soy sauce, sherry, ginger and spring onions. Rub the duck well with the mixture and let it soak for about half an hour.

Heat the fat in a pan and fry the duck until a light brown. Replace it in a heavy pot, pour in the soy mixture and 3 cups of water, then

Duck

heat it over a big fire until boiling. Reduce the heat and simmer for 1 hour. Add the sugar and boil for another ½ hour. The time required for this recipe depends on the tenderness of the bird. Another ½ hour may be needed if the bird is tough.

紅 燒 栗 子 鴨
Braised Duck With Chestnuts

1 large duck	1 cup soy sauce
½ lb. chestnuts	1 spring onion
¼ lb. mushrooms	2—3 slices ginger
½ lb. pork	

Wash the duck carefully and cut into about one inch cubes.

Soak the chestnuts in hot water for ½ hour and peel off the outer and inner skins, cut the pork into cubes, and the spring onion into sections. Soak the mushrooms in warm water for 10 minutes.

Then place the pieces of duck in a large covered saucepan made of thick metal with the pork cubes, mushrooms, onion, ginger and chestnuts. Add the soy sauce and 3 cups of water, then bring to the boil. Simmer over a low fire for 1½ hours. A longer time may be needed if the meat is not tender.

酒 燉 鴨
Wine-Simmered Duck

1 fat duck	2—4 slices ginger
1 lb. sherry	1 t-sp aniseed powder
4 tb-sp salt	1 spring onion

Singe and wash the duck thoroughly. Rub the inside with salt and aniseed powder. Put the spring onion, ginger and the remaining salt in the duck. Place the duck and wine in a heavy pot and heat on a low fire and simmer continuously for 3 hours. Remove it from the pot and wait until it is cold and firm. Dissect the legs, wings and breast first then cut them into pieces. Lay the neck at the bottom of the plate as a foundation and finally put the meat of the legs and breast on top. Serve with raw spring onion if desired. This dish goes marvellously with wine.

烤 鴨
Roast Duck

1 duck	2 tb-sp salt
1 cup sherry	

Duck

Pluck and wash the duck till it is thoroughly clean. Remove the oil sacs. Place it in a heavy pot with salt and wine. Cook on a low fire for ½ hour. Remove from the pot and place in an oven and bake in a moderate oven for about 20 minutes or until the duck is brown. Stick a fork throuhg the duck. It will easily go through if it is done.

Serve with sweet soy jam if available.

神 仙 鴨
Fairy Duck

1 duck	½ t-sp cinnamon or
6 tb-sp soy sauce	aniseed powder
2 cups sherry	2—3 slices ginger
½ t-sp sugar	1 spring onion

Pluck and clean the duck. Cut off the oil sacs and cut the duck into 1½ inches squares. Place in an iron heavy pot with the sherry, soy sauce, spring onion, sugar and ginger. Cover tightly and simmer a low fire for 20 minutes. Turn off the fire but leave the lid on. After 15 minutes cook over a low fire for 15 minutes. Again, turn off the fire and after 10 minutes cook for another 15 minutes. Keep the lid tightly on for 30 minutes before serving.

The recipe is very economical as regards the use of fuel, because the cooking is not continuous. Before the duck is placed in the pot be sure that there is no water in it as the duck should only be cooked with wine and soy sauce.

南 京 版 鴨
Nanking Salt-Water Duck

1 fat duck	1 t-sp Szechuan pepper or
4 tb-sp salt	cinnamon

Pluck, clean and draw as usual. In China, Szechuam pepper in the form of unground seeds, used. Cinnamon provides a satisfactory substitute. Put the salt and Szechuan pepper or cinnamon in a pan and mix briskly for one minute over a low fire. Wait until it is cold then rub the mixture hard over both outside and the inside of the duck. Leave it for four or five days in a cool place or in the refrigerator, then dry it under the sun for a day or two. In a really cold climate it will keep even longer than a month but in a tropical climate, of course, the refrigerator keeps it quite satisfactory for a while.

Duck

When it is ready to be cooked, rinse off the salt, then insert two pairs of chopsticks into the duck from the back of the tail—this is a good way to absorb the heat. Heat four pints of water in a boiler over a big fire until boiling, then put in the duck and boil for 15 minutes. Cover tight and do not take the duck out until the water is cold.

An excellent way to serve the duck is to dissect it into legs, wings, back and breast then to further chop each section into pieces. Lay the neck and bones at the bottom of the plate and the meat on top. This way of serving duck cold goes particularly well with either European wine or the Chinese wine that is drunk warm from a little porcelain bowl. The duck shops in Nanking are specialists of this dish.

八 寶 全 鴨
Eight-Precious Duck

1 fat duck	2 tb-sp pearl barley
½ cup glutinous rice	1 cup fresh chestnuts
½ cup lotus seeds	4 slices fresh ginger
¼ cup raisins	1 t-sp salt
¼ cup white nuts	3 spring onions
2 t-sp sugar	½ cup soy sauce
¼ cup candied jujubes	2 tb-sp sherry (optional)

Wash the duck thoroughly and remove all the inner parts by making a 1½ inches slit at the back of the tail.

Soak the chestnuts, white nuts and lotus seeds in hot water, then shell them or peel off the skins. Boil the rice and barley until cooked.

Then mix the barley, rice, with white nuts, lotus seeds, jujubes, chestnuts, raisins, ¼ cup soy sauce and salt. Stuff them in the duck and place in a heavy pot. Put 3 cups of water in the pot with ¼ cup soy sauce, sherry, spring onions and ginger.

Heat over a hot fire until the water boils, turn low and simmer for 1½ hours. Add sugar and boil for ½ hour longer.

The time may be lengthened or reduced slightly according to the tenderness of the meat. Place on an oval plate and serve hot.

炸 糯 米 全 鴨

Fried Stuffed Duck With Glutinous Rice

1 fat duck
2 cups glutinous rice (cooked)
2 tb-sp sherry (optional)
1 oz. spring onion
3--4 slices fresh ginger

1 t-sp syrup
1 lb. cooking oil
1 t-sp salt
3 tb-sp soy sauce

Clean the duck thoroughly and remove the oil sacs. Make a cut about 1½ inches long at the back of the tail and draw the bird.

Wash the rice and cook it in the usual way. Mix the syrup, sherry, soy sauce, chopped ginger and spring onion. Soak the duck for one hour in the mixture. Hang the duck up for 4 hours until the skin is dry. Stuff the glutinous rice, salt, ginger, spring onion and remaining soy sauce in the duck then heat the cooking oil till smoking hot. Put the duck in the pan and fry in deep oil until it is brown and crispy. Place it on an oval place and serve hot.

子 薑 炒 鴨 絲

Fried Duck Shreds With Ginger

1 duck
2 oz. fresh ginger (young)
1 t-sp salt
1 tb-sp cornflour

2 tb-sp soy sauce
2 tb-sp sherry (optional)
1 spring onion
4 tb-sp lard or cooking oil

Wash and clean the duck but cut only the breast meat and legs into shreds. Save the rest of the duck for soup or other dishes.

Peel off the skin of the ginger and cut into shreds and chop the onion into pieces. Mix the soy souce, sherry cornflour, salt and onion pieses with duck shreds.

Heat 3 tb-sp fat in a skillet till hot, put the seasoned duck shreds in and after stirring for 1 minute take it out.

Heat another tablespoonful of fat till hot, then stir in the ginger shreds for 1 minute. Add the duck shreds and stir together for another 2 minutes. Serve it piping hot.

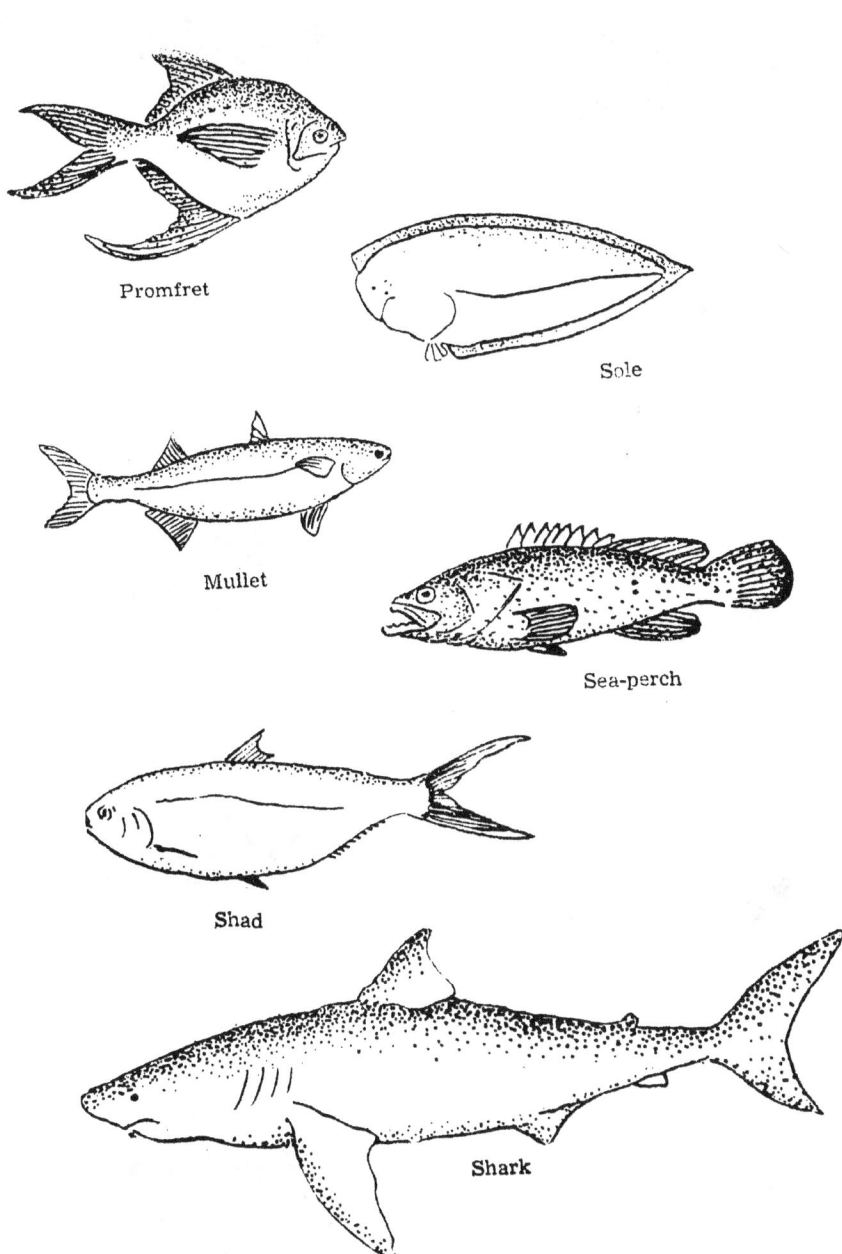

Cuttle Fish.

Squid

Common Herring

Haddock

Sardine

Scup

Cod

Bass

Eel

Carp

Fish

魚
Chapter 3. Fish

Cooking fish in the Chinese way involves the use of wine, ginger, vinegar and spring onion to get rid of the undesirable smell of the fish. To know how to select the best fish in the market is as important as learning how to cook the fish. Some fish have scales but some have not. They should not have a disagreeable smell. Their eyes should be crystal clear and their gills rosy in colour. When a scaly fish is selected, the scales must be firm on the fish. If a fish has a wide gaping mouth with its gill flaps open, it can safely be assumed that the fish is very fresh. As the freshness of the fish goes off, the fish loses its appearance; the eyes become dull and the flesh becomes so soft that if the tip of a finger is pressed on the fish its impression will remain, the gill flaps will become brownish. All these are signs of staleness.

In China there are two kinds of fish, river or fresh water fish and sea fish. River fish play a much greater part, probably because the Chinese method of cooking has made it so. Of river fish there are the carp, buffalo carp, bream and some others which have no equivalent name in English. Of sea fish, blue-fish, white-fish, flounder, cod, salmon, bass, skatfish, fresh sardine, scup, butter-fish, plaice, sole and turbot are good for Chinese dishes,. Sea fish is more used along the coasal provinces but when caught and salted, are available for people living far inland. Some fish are of both types. Shad, mullet and perch are partly sea and partly river fish. The shad is a great delicacy in China. The eel is a beautiful fish with a good reputation as food. The flesh is well flavoured but it is very bony. Terrapin belongs to the same family as the turtle. Its flesh is delicious and is considered very nutritious especially for women.

If a fish is desired to be steamed or braised in whole do not cut off the fins, tail and head. First scale the fish from tail to head. With a sharp knife make a small opening in the belly and remove the entrails. Wash the fish with a little salt so that the blood membrane can be removed. Drain and wait till the skin becomes dry before cooking because the skin might stick on the frying pan if it is wet. To serve a whole fish on an oval plate is the traditional custom in most of the Chinese restaurants and homes.

When a fish is to be cooked in slices the fish may or may not be skinned. To skin a fish, take a litte salt between the thumb and fingers and gently pull the skin from the head towards the tail.

Fish

An eel is always killed by the fishermen in the market. Wash with lukewarm water so that the fishy smell can be washed away. Turtle is killed at home. Lay the back of the turtle on the ground; as soon as it stretches out its head cut it off at once. Pour boiling water on it and pull away it's skin. Separate its back and body then remove the entrails. Sometimes it is cooked whole and sometimes in pieces according to the particular recipe

清 蒸 鰣 魚
Steamed Shad

1 shad (2 or 3 lbs.)
2 tb-sp lard
2 tb-sp soy sauce

6 slices ginger
1 spring onion
2 t-sp salt

Wash the shad and leave the scales on. Cut it into sections. Place the pieces in a bowl or deep plate and add the seasonings. Put the bowl in a boiler and steam for 15 minutes with the lid on tightly after the water starts to boil. Mix a little soy sauce, vinegar and chopped ginger to be dipped into while eating.

Never remove the scales of the shad for they can be removed at the time they are eaten. If the scales are removed before they are cooked, the skin will become dryish and the taste will be different. Moreover, in China it is a traditional custom to steam the shad rather than use any other method. Shad is very rare in the Chinese market and is rather expensive.

紅 燒 鰣 魚
Braised Shad

1 shad (2 or 3 lbs.)
2 tb-sp lard
4 tb-sp soy sauce
2 tb-sp sherry (optional)
1 cup chicken soup

2 ozs. fresh lard
6 slices ginger
1 spring onion
1 t-sp salt

Prepare the shad as in the preceding recipe. Heat the lard and fry the shad for 5 minutes. Add the sliced ginger, spring onion and sherry and cover the lid for 2 minutes. Then add salt, chicken soup and soy sauce and cook for about 15 minutes and serve.

Fish

冬菰蒸魚塊
Steamed Fish Slices

1 lb. plaice, sole or turbot	Few slices ham
1 oz. mushroom	1 tb-sp vinegar
2—3 slices ginger	1 tb-sp soy sauce
1 t-sp salt	2 tb-sp lard
	½ t-sp sugar

Cut the mushrooms and spring onions into slices and the ginger into shreds. Mix them with soy sauce. Wash the fish thoroughly and cut it into large slices. Rub with salt and place in a basin with the white side up. Cover it with the other ingredients, put the basin in a steamer with the lid on and steam for 15 minutes. Season with a drop of vinegar, pepper and salt before serving in a big Chinese bowl or soup plate.

肉餡魚
Meat Stuffed Fish

1½ or 2 lbs. fish	½ cup soy sauce
4 ozs meat	2—3 spring onions
1 t-sp sugar	2—3 slices ginger
4 tb-sp cooking oil	½ tb-sp cornflour

Clean the fish and make some slashes crosswise on the back of the fish. Chop or mince the meat with spring onion and ginger, mix with 1 tb-sp soy sauce, ½ tb-sp cornflour and 2 tb-sp water and stuff them into the belly of the fish. Heat the cooking oil till smoking and fry the fish on both sides until brown. Add in the remaining soy sauce, sugar and 1 cup of water. Cover the skillet and cook over a medium fire for about 15 minutes. Red snapper or scup is best suited for this kind of cooking.

煎鹹魚
Fried Salted Fish

½ lb. salted haddock or any other kind of salted fish	1 t-sp sugar
4 tb-sp cooking oil	2—3 slices ginger

Wash the salted fish. Clean and remove the scales. Cut it into pieces. Heat the oil till hot, then fry them until they are brown. Chop the ginger and put into the frying pan and fry the fish for one more minutes. Add 1 t-sp of sugar on top of the fish according to individual taste.

Fish

Salted fish is always available in the markets. It is good to eat as an accompanying dish with white congee. Sick people without appetite and unable to eat rich food always use salted fish.

炒 冬 菰 魚 片
Fried Fish With Mushrooms

1 lb. any round fish	2 spring onions
2 tb-sp flour	2 ozs mushrooms
1 bamboo shoot	6 tb-sp lard
½ t-sp salt	2 tb-sp soy sauce

Slice the fish into thin pieces, and dip into a thin flour paste. Cut the spring onions and bamboo shoots into slices. Wash the mushrooms and cut off the stems. Soak them in ½ cup of water, before cooking. Fry the bamboo shoots and mushrooms with half amount of lard and ½ t-sp salt. Then put them away after having stirred constantly for 3 minutes. Heat the remaining lard till smoking hot and drop the fish in and fry gently, put back the bamboo shoots and mushrooms, together with the mushrooms water and soy sauce; braise for 1 minute with the lid on and then it will be ready to be served when every slice of the fish turns white.

炸 魚 片
Deep-Fried Fish

1 lb. white fish	1 t-sp salt
½ lb. cooking oil	2 ozs flour
1 egg	

Clean the fish well, remove everything inside. Rub with ½ t-sp salt. Mix the flour, egg and the remaining salt and coat the fish. Bring ½ lb. cooking oil to boil and drop the fish in five or six at a time and fry them until brown. Then remove from fire and drain. Serve with salt and pepper.

Sprats or small herring are best suited for this cooking.

紅 燒 鯉 魚
Braised Carp

1 carp (about 2 lbs.)	1 oz. spring onion
3 tb-sp soy sauce	2 tb-sp sherry (optional)
4 tb-sp cooking oil or lard	1 t-sp sugar
	1 t-sp salt
5—6 slices ginger	

Fish

Scale and wash the fish thoroughly. Allow it to dry for a few minutes and rub it with salt. Heat the lard and fry each side for about 5 minutes and keep pouring the oil on every part. Pour on the fish 3 tb-sp of soy sauce, pieces of ginger, sectioned spring onions and braise for 3 minutes so that the seasoning can penetrate the fish. Add a cup of water and cook for 10 minutes. Finally, add in the sherry and sugar and cook for 5 minutes more.

Fish cooked with soy sauce is one of the most popular forms of fish dishes in China. Carp, bream, scup, mullet and perch are suitable for this kind of cooking.

紅 燒 鱔 魚

Braised Eel

1 lb. eel	6 buds garlic
1 t-sp cornflour	½ t-sp sugar
2 tb-sp soy sauce	½ t-sp salt
2 tb-sp sherry (optional)	3 tb-sp lard

Kill the eels. Cut them first into two inch sections and then into shreds. Wash them thoroughly. Heat the lard; then fry them for 5 minutes. Add the sherry, sugar, soy sauce, salt, garlic and a cup of water and simmer with the lid on for another 15 minutes. Pour in the cornflour water and stir well. Sprinkle with pepper and serve.

炒 鱔 魚 絲

Fried Eel

1 lb. eel	4 tb-sp sherry (optional)
4 tb-sp soy sauce	1 t-sp sugar
6 tb-sp lard	1 t-sp cornflour

Kill and shred the eels. Wash them clean. Heat the lard till hot and fry the eel till brown; then add the wine, soy sauce and ½ cup of water. Cover the lid tight and simmer for 10 minutes. Mix sugar, cornflour and a little water and pour into the pan. Stir well and mix thoroughly. Season with sesame oil while serving if desired.

紅 燒 甲 魚

Braised Turtle

1 turtle	4 tb-sp sherry (optional)
½ lb. pork	8 tb-sp soy sauce
4 tb-sp lard	1 t-sp salt
½ lb. cooking oil	1 t-sp sugar

Fish

Kill the turtle. Cut it into pieces and put in the frying pan. Heat over a low fire until dry, or all the moisture has evaporated. Heat the cooking oil, and fry the turtle until a light brown. Drain and save the oil, Add wine, soy sauce, lard and 1 cup of water. Heat until it boils again. Cut the pork into pieces and put them with the turtle in a heavy boiler and simmer on a low fire for 2 hours. Add salt and sugar and cook for 10 minutes before serving.

清蒸甲魚
Steamed Turtle

1 turtle	½ tb-sp salt
½ lb. bamboo shoots	2—3 slices ginger
2 ozs fresh lard	4 tb-sp sherry (optional)

Kill the turtle and wash with boiling water. Cut the breast crosswise and draw the turtle. Put diced ginger, sliced bamboo shoots, salt and wine inside the turtle. Place it into a bowl and steam for 2 hours. Serve hot.

魚丸
Fish Balls

1½ fish	½ t-sp salt
2 t-sp cornflour	1 t-sp pepper

Remove the head of the fish, then split it from the back into 2 halves. With a spoon, scrape the inside of the fish from the tail toward the head. Do not scrape in the reverse direction as then the fine bones will turn loose and the meat cannot be scraped out. Chop the fish finely. Dissolve the salt in a cup of water and add it gradually to the meat. Add the pepper and cornflour and mix them thoroughly, then take a fistful of the seasoned fish and squeeze it out through the hole formed by the index finger and the thumb and scoop with a spoon. In this way fish balls will be formed. Put them into hot water and boil them for 3 minutes. They can be stored in refrigerator for days. They may be fried in deep oil until brown and served with a sweet and sour sauce and pickles. They may be cooked with mushrooms, bamboo shoots, etc. And they can also be added to chicken soup or meat soup or to the soup in which the fish balls are cooked. With 1½ t-sp salt and 1 tb-sp of lard in addition to a few cabbage hearts, mushrooms and bamboo shoots it would make a nice delicious soup.

Fish

蒸 全 魚
Steamed Fish (Whole)

1 fish	Few slices ham
1 t-sp salt	2 tb-sp soy sauce
2 tb-sp lard or cooking oil	5 slices fresh ginger
8 mushrooms	1 spring onion

Scale the fish and rub with salt. Put in a bowl or big plate; then add all the seasonings except the spring onions. Arrange the mushrooms and ham on top of the fish. Steam about 15 minutes and add the spring onions before serving.

River perch and sea perch are good for this dish.

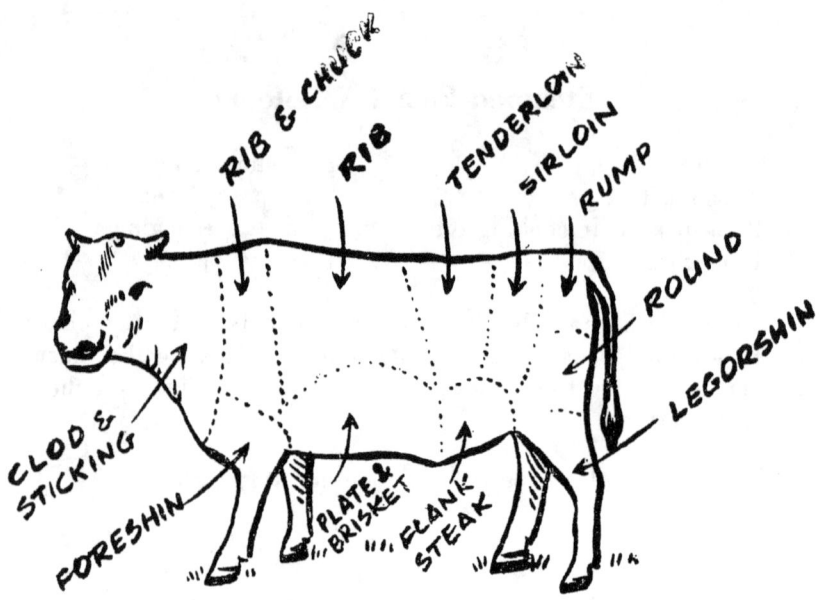

Beef Cuts

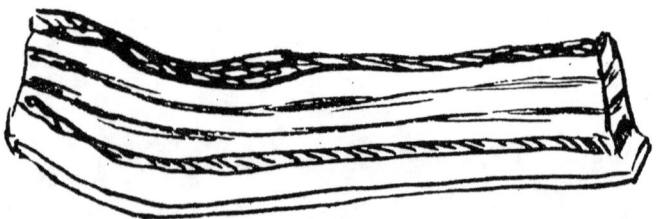

Streaky Pork or five-flowered pork

Meat

肉
Chapter 4. Meat
猪 肉
Pork

When pork is selected in the market see that the skin of the pork is thin. If the skin is thick it is tough and takes a longer time to cook regardless of whatever method is employed. Also see that the meat is thick in colour but not too red nor too pale.

Pork is braised sometimes with the skin and sometimes without it, but it is never used in frying. Great care should be taken to remove all hairs. The skin is quite tasty if properly braised.

Timing is important and depends primarily on the size and shape of the pieces as well as the method employed.

When a whole piece of pork is stewed or braised a longer cooking time will be needed then when braised or stewed in pieces. When a piece of lean pork is braised or stewed a little cooking oil should be used to fry the pork first before soy sauce and water are added. Always add sugar when the meat is about done otherwise the meat will be burned easily for sugar will make the gravy sticky and dry. To test whether the meat is done or not use a chopstick or a fork to stick through the pork. If it is done the stick goes through easily otherwise cook over a low fire a little longer and add a little water if necessary.

For both braising and white cooking a low fire must be employed and a heavy pot should be used so that the materials cooked will not be burned and the gravy will get dried, for once the gravy is dried up the original taste and the nutritious value of the material will be decreased. In the plain braised pork in pieces other accessories such as fresh vegetables, salt or dried sea food are often added. The duration of the cooking depends on the nature of the materials cooked. For instance when spinach is added to the braised pork 5 extra minutes will only be needed; for cabbage 10 to 20 minutes and for potatoes 30 minutes.

For frying always cut the meat against grain. First take a piece of meat and slice it thinly then cut into slices or shreds. The differences between braising and frying are:

1. Always use a low fire for braising and a high fire for frying.
2. For frying the materials are always cut into pieces and in braising they are sometimes braised in whole pieces.

Meat

3. Frying needs a shorter time; sometimes only a few minutes.

In China cleavers are used to chop the meat. First cut the meat into pieces and then into slices, slices into shreds and shreds into mince. In countries other than China a grinder of medium size should be used for grinding meat. The best cuts for meat balls are those with a little fat in them, such as pork chop. Skin and tendon should never be ground. If the meat is too lean the cake or the meat ball will be too dry and stiff Ground meat is almost always made into balls or cakes. Meat balls can form a dish alone or in company with other dishes.

紅燒猪蹄
Braised Pork Leg (Whole)

3 lbs. pork leg
1 cup soy sauce
1 t-sp salt
¼ cup sherry (or without)
1 t-sp sugar

Select the middle cut of the pork leg and wash it. Make a few slashes on the skin. Put it in a heavy pot with soy sauce, salt, sherry and two rice bowls of water. Cover the lid tightly and heat over a hot fire till boiling then turn to a low fire and simmer for 3 hours. Add the sugar and heat for ½ hour more. Place the whole piece on a big plate and serve with rice.

紅燒肉
Braised Pork (Whole)

2 lbs. pork
1 cup soy sauce
½ t-sp salt
¼ cup sherry (or without)
1 t-sp sugar
2-3 spring onions
2 slices ginger

Select an excellent piece of tenderloin or shoulder not too fat. Carefully wash and drain off all the moisture. Place in the pot a bowl of water and all the above ingredients except sugar. Simmer slowly for about 2 hours, then add the sugar and boil continually for ½ hour more. Cut the pork in thin slices when cold and arrange on a serving plate. Pour the gravy on top of the meat and serve with rice.

紅燒肉塊
Braised Pork (Pieces)

2 lbs. pork
1 cup soy sauce
1 t-sp sherry (or without)
2 tb-sp cooking oil
1 t-sp sugar

Meat

Wash the meat. Cut into 1 or 1½ inch cubes. Heat the oil and fry the pork and turn constantly till a light brown. Put meat and the soy sauce in a heavy pot and cook for 1 minute. Stir continuously while cooking. Add one bowl of water and heat over a big fire till boiling. When it boils, add sherry and ginger. Cover the pan tightly and cook over a very low fire for 1½ hours; then add sugar and continue to simmer for ½ hour.

This dish can be mixed or cooked with cabbages, eggs, turnips, abalone, bamboo shoots, squid or salted haddock.

紅 燒 猪 肉 排
Braised Pork Chop

2 lbs. pork chop	½ cup soy sauce
1 t-sp sugar	½ lb. cooking oil

Get from the butcher the pork chop which has already been cut into pieces about a ¼ inch thick. Wash them and drain away all the extra moisture.

Heat the cooking oil and fry the pork chops in several lots until each piece is brown on both sides. Remove from fire and leave 2 tb-sp of oil in a heavy boiler and put back the fried pork chop with soy sauce and 1 cup of water. Heat on a high fire till boiling, then simmer for 1 hour on a low fire. Add sugar and cook for ½ hour and serve.

The gravy is very tasty especially if it is mixed with vegetables. Fry ½ lb. of spinach or cabbage with a little oil first, and put the braised pork chop on the top and then pour on the gravy. This dish is considered to be one of the most delicious dishes to eat with rice.

紅 燒 白 菜 猪 肉
Braised Pork With Cabbage

1 lb. cabbage	½ cup soy sauce
1 lb. pork	1 t-sp sugar
2 oz. mushrooms	4 tb-sp cooking oil
½ cup dried shrimps	

Wash the cabbage thoroughly and drain off all surplus moisture. Cut it into squares and the pork into 1 inch cubes. The pork selected should be fairly lean. The mushrooms and dried shrimps should have been previously soaked in hot water, the water in which the mushrooms and shrimps have been soaked being reserved for further cooking.

Meat

Place 2 lb-sp of cooking oil in a deep pan and add the pork when it is hot. Pour in the soy sauce and 1 bowl of water. After 1 hour add the cabbage and cook for about 10 minutes until the cabbage turns to a rich red colour. Remove the contents of the pan from the fire and place them on one side. Add the balance of the cooking oil and heat to smoking hot; quickly add the soaked mushrooms and shrimps and bring to boiling point. Replace cabbage, pork and mushroom water; cover the pan tightly and cook under a low fire for about 30 minutes until the cabbage is thoroughly done.

紅 燒 松 子 豬 肉
Braised Pork With Pine-Nuts

1 lb. fresh pork
½ cup soy sauce
3 oz. pine-nuts
1 t-sp sugar
2 tb-sp cooking oil

Select an evenly lean piece of fresh pork and with a sharp knife cut it into cubes about one inch square. Over a hot fire fry the pieces of pork with the cooking oil for about five minutes, turning frequently. Add one pint of boiling water, the soy sauce, and pinenuts. Simmer the whole slowly until the pork is tender.

In the cool weather this makes a most excellent dish to be eaten with rice and has the advantage of being appetizing when served either hot or cold. Cabbage, which has been previously boiled and carefully drained, and on which the liquid from the above dish has been poured while piping hot, will be found to be a most delicious accompanying dish.

紅 燒 橄 欖 豬 肉
Braised Pork With Olive

1 lb. pork leg (with skin)
¼ cup sherry (optional)
¼ cup soy sauce
2 oz. rock sugar or sugar
10 olives

Wash the pork and cut into 1½ inch cubes. Put in a heavy pot with 1½ cups of water. Heat over a hot fire until boiling. Skim the scum if any, add half of the wine and simmer on a low fire for ½ hour. Pour in the soy sauce and the remaining wine. The pork will be nearly done in about 1½ hours. Make a few dissections on the olives lengthwise from one end to the other. Add them and the sugar into the pot to cook with the pork for 10 minutes. If fresh olives are not obtainable, preserved olives in cans or bottles can be used as well but the length of time for cooking should be shortened from 10 to 5 minutes. This dish is delicious and its smell is fragrant.

Meat

燻 豬 肉
Smoked Pork

1 lb. pork leg
1 tb-sp salt
6 tb-sp sherry (optional)
6 tb-sp soy sauce
½ lb. saw dust
1 t-sp aniseed powder

Wash the pork and boil in ½ pint of water for about 10 minutes after the water has started to boil. Add the sherry and heat for another 10 minutes. Pour in the salt and of soy sauce and simmer for another 20 minutes. Remove from fire.

Put the saw dust and aniseed powder in a heavy iron or brass pan. Place the pan on the fire. Put the pork on an iron frame or grate on the top of the saw dust and smoke with the lid on until brown. Turn occasionally while smoking. Cut into the thin slices and serve with soy sauce.

Do not boil the pork too soft as it is then not good for smoking.

叉 燒 肉
Barbecued Pork

1 lb. lean pork
½ t-sp salt
1 t-sp sugar
½ tb-sp soy sauce
1 t-sp sherry (optional)
1 tb-sp honey
2 cloves crushed garlic
(or without)

Cut the pork along the grain about 2 inches wide. Rub with salt and sugar and allow it to stand for 2 hours. Mix thoroughly soy sauce, sherry, crushed garlic and honey and rub into the meat.

Heat oven to moderate and roast for 10 minutes. Turn the meat over, raise the heat, baste with a little cooked peanut or vegetable oil and roast another 15 minutes. Slice each strip against grain into ¼ inch thick pieces.

烤 豬 肉
Roast Pork

5 lbs. pork
2 tb-sp salt
1 oz. sesame oil
8 tb-sp soy sauce
2 t-sp aniseed powder

Wash the pork and drain well. Use a sharp knife to scratch the skin of the pork to make it thinner. Rub the pork with salt, soy sauce, sesame oil and aniseed powder. Put in an oven and roast on a medium heat until the skin is brown and crisp. While roasting spread a little sesame oil on the skin; repeat it several times. Turn while roasting. Cut the roasted pork into slices and serve with soy sauce and sesame oil.

In China or in any big Chinese restaurant the pork is roasted on a charcoal fire and huge iron fork is used to hold the pork when roasting.

蒸 猪 肉
Steamed Minced Pork

½ lb. pork
2 eggs
1 tb-sp lard
½ t-sp sugar

2—3 spring onions
½ t-sp salt
1 tb-sp cornflour
1 tb-sp soy sauce

The pork selected should be fairly lean. Mince the meat finely and put into a bowl with the beaten eggs. Season with salt, lard, soy sauce, sugar and chopped spring onions. Dissolve the cornflour in 2 tb-sp water and mix in the pork cake. Place the bowl in a steamer and steam over a moderate heat with the lid on for 20 minutes. Serve with pepper.

白 切 肉
White-Cut Meat

½ cup soy sauce
2 lbs. pork

2 t-sp ground ginger

The pork selected should have more lean meat than fat. The best suitable piece for this dish is the leg (middle cut), or pork chop. If it is pork chop remove the bones. Pour 1½ pints of water in a pot and put the pork. Heat continuously over a hot fire for 40 minutes. Remove from fire and cut into thin slices when it is cold. Serve with soy sauce and ground ginger.

焦 鹽 肉
Sweet And Salted Pork

3 lbs. pork
½ cup sherry (optional)

2 tb-sp salt
4 oz. rock sugar (or sugar)

Wash the pork and cut into squares. Put the pieces into a pot with sherry and heat until it boils. Add the salt and 1 bowl of water.

Meat

Simmer over a low fire for 2 hours. Mix in the rock sugar and cook for 10 minutes or more until the sugar is melted.

The pork selected for this dish can be either lean or fat. The leg is best for lean meat and streaky meat for the fat.

蒸 鹹 肉
Steamed Bacon

1 lb. bacon
½ t-sp sugar   1 tb-sp sherry (optional)

Place the whole piece of bacon in a deep bowl or basin and steam it with sugar and sherry for half an hour in a steamer. Cut it in oblong pieces when serving. The steamed bacon is not as salty as fried bacon because the steam goes into the bacon itself.

After the bacon is steamed it can also be fried with celery if desired. Cut about ½ lb. of celery into slices and fry with the bacon for 5 minutes in 1 tb-sp of lard. Add 1 tb-sp water and cook for 2 or 3 minutes. Serve after water has evaporated.

蒸 火 腿
Steamed Ham

1½ lbs. ham   1 oz. rock sugar or sugar
1 tb-sp sherry (optional)

Wash the ham and leave it as a whole piece. Put it in a bowl and steam it for 1 hour. Add the sherry and steam for another ½ hour, then add the sugar. After continuously steaming for 20 minutes, it is ready for serving.

If Chinese ham, which is more salty, is used, put in slightly more sugar.

鹹 魚 蒸 肉
Steamed Minced Meat With Salted Fish

3/4 lb. pork   1 t-sp chopped ginger
2 tb-sp soy sauce   1 tb-sp cornflour
¼ lb. salted fish (any kind)   1 t-sp sugar
2 tb-sp lard

Meat

Grind the pork and mix well with the ingredients (with the exception of sugar and lard) and 1 tb-sp water into large cake and place in a bowl.

Wash the fish and cut into pieces. Arrange on the top of the meat cake, sprinkle the sugar on top of the fish and add the lard. Steam for 15 minutes after the water starts to boil.

飯蒸肉
Steamed Pork In Rice

Rice (depends on the
No. of persons)
1 lb. pork lean

3 tb-sp salt
4 tb-sp sherry

Rub the pork with the salt and let it stay over night. Wash the pork and put it in a bowl of sherry and then put the bowl into a boiler before cooking the rice. Cover the bowl with a larger bowl so that the rice water will not splash into the pork. Wash the rice and pour into the same boiler with water on top of the bowl. When the rice is cooked the meat is done also. This dish is called Steamed Fresh Salted Pork in Rice. The advantage of this method of cooking is that it saves time and fuel. If desired, the pork can be steamed separately without cooking the rice. Put the bowl into the boiler with water about 3 inches in height and steam on a low fire for about 1 hour. Cut the pork into slices and serve.

粉蒸肉
Steamed Pork With Rice Powder

2 lbs. pork leg (middle cut)
6 tb-sp soy sauce
6 tb-sp sherry (optional)

3 slices spring onions
1 bowl glutinous rice powder
or rice powder

Wash the pork and cut into oblong pieces. Mix with soy sauce, sherry, and chopped spring onion. Add the powder and mix thoroughly. The ground rice should be baked slightly before mixing with the pork. Put in basin or bowl and steam with the lid covered for 2 hours over a low fire after boiling. During the process of steaming turn the meat over several times and add a few drops of water if necessary.

Meat

冬菰餡肉
Meat Stuffed Mushrooms

1 lb. mushrooms (big ones)	1 tb-sp soy sauce
½ lb. ground pork	1 tb-sp cornflour
1 t-sp salt	1 tb-sp sherry (optional)
	3 tb-sp cooking oil

Cut off the stems of the mushrooms and save them for soup. Mix the ground meat, soy sauce, salt, cornflour and sherry thoroughly and stuff in the caps of each mushroom enough to form a smooth round hump.

Heat the oil till hot and fry the stuffed mushrooms with the meat on top for 5 minutes and then arrange them in a bowl and steam them with 2 cups of water for 5-10 minutes from the time the water boils. The length of time depends on the size of the mushrooms. Take them out and put on a serving plate.

炸粉肉片
Fried Pork Cutlets In Batter

1½ lbs. pork cutlets	4 eggs
1 tb-sp sherry (optional)	1 t-sp pepper
1 cup flour	1½ t-sp salt
4 cups cooking oil	

Cut the pork cutlets into cubes about an inch square 2 hours before cooking. Put the meat in a deep bowl and pour the sherry over to which has been added 1½ t-sp salt.

When ready to cook make a batter with flour and add in the well-beaten eggs and a very small quantity of water if the mixture is too stiff. Heat the oil to boiling point and quickly immerse each cube of pork in the batter and drop into the deep oil. Remove from fire and drain off the extra oil. Sprinkle with pepper while serving.

糯米刺毛丸
Glutinous Rice Pork Balls

1 lb. pork	2—3 spring onions
½ lb. glutinous rice	2 t-sp cornflour
1 t-sp salt	2 eggs
2 tb-sp sherry (optional)	1 t-sp sugar
2—3 slices ginger	2 tb-sp soy sauce

The pork selected should not be too fat. Wash the glutinous rice and soak it over night. The meat should be chopped or ground very fine and the same must be done with the ginger and the spring onions. Add the cornflour, beaten eggs, 1 t-sp salt, sugar, sherry, soy sauce, 1 tb-sp water, ground ginger and chopped spring onion to the chopped pork. After mixing thoroughly the meat paste, add ½ cup of water and mix again for a while. Make the meat paste into balls each about the size of an egg. Drain the rice and roll the meat balls on the rice so that the rice will stick on the balls. Arrange them on a big bowl and steam for 1 hour.

紅 燒 白 菜 肉 丸
Pork Meat Balls With Cabbage

1 lb. cabbage
1½ lbs. pork (lean)
½ lb. pork (fat)
½ cup soy sauce
½ lb. cooking oil

2—3 slices ginger
4 spring onions
1 tb-sp cornflour
1 t-sp salt
2 eggs

The meat should be chopped or ground very fine and the same must be done with ginger and spring onion. Add the cornflour, beaten eggs, ½ t-sp salt and ground spring onion and ginger to the pork. After mixing thoroughly the meat paste, add ½ cup of water and mix again for a while. Make the meat paste into small balls each about twice as big as an egg.

Heat the cooking oil till smoking and fry the meat balls until a golden brown. Remove from fire and pour off the oil leaving only 2 tb-sp in a saucepan. Place the meat balls on the top of the raw cabbage, add soy sauce, ½ t-sp salt, 1 cup of water and cook over a slow fire until the cabbage is soft and done. Arrange the cabbage on a plate and put the meat balls on top. Add the gravy in which it was cooked. Serve hot.

豆 腐 猪 肉 丸
Fried Bean Curd And Pork Balls

4 pieces bean curd
1 lb. pork
8 tb-sp cooking oil
1 t-sp salt
1 tb-sp soy sauce

1 tb-sp sherry (optional)
1 spring onion
½ t-sp sugar
1 tb-sp cornflour

Meat

Chop the meat very finely and mix with the smashed bean curd. Chop the spring onion and mix it in also. Add the soy sauce, salt, sherry and cornflour. Mix thoroughly and make them into small sized balls. Heat the oil till smoking and fry the balls until they are brown. Add sugar, ¼ cup water and soy sauce and cook for 10 minutes. Serve with pepper.

炸 肉 丸
Fried Pork Balls

1 lb. pork	1 t-sp black pepper
3 tb-sp soy sauce	2 tb-sp flour
2 eggs	1—2 spring onion
1 t-sp sugar	1 lb. cooking oil
½ t-sp salt	

With a sharp cleaver and chopping board chop the fresh meat. This is preferable to putting it through a grinder. Chop the spring onion very fine and add to the mixture soy sauce, salt, sugar, flour, 2 eggs and ½ cup of water.

Between the palms make balls, smaller than an egg. Heat the cooking oil to the proper temperature for deep-frying and fry the meat balls till brown and crispy. Remove, drain off the oil and place on a serving dish. Sprinkle with black pepper.

紅 燒 獅 子 頭
Braised Lion's Head

1½ lbs. pork (lean)	4 spring onions
½ lb. pork (fat)	1 t-sp cornflour
¼ cup soy sauce	2 eggs
1½ t-sp salt	½ lb. spinach
2—3 slices ginger	

The method used should be the same as for meat balls but the difference is that Lion's Head is bigger than meat balls. In other words they are big meat balls. After mixing the meat paste with all the seasonings except the soy sauce make it into 4 big balls.

Fry them in hot oil as in the case of meat balls. Remove them from the fire and add soy sauce and 1 cup of water and cook over a low fire for about ½ hour.

Meat

Wash the spinach and cut into sections if necessary. Drain the extra moisture and fry with 2 tb-sp of oil for 1 minute. Warm up the Lion's Head and put on the top of the fried spinach and serve.

This dish is famous in Chekiang.

芹 菜 炒 肉 絲
Fried Pork Shreds With Celery

½ lb. pork
1 tb-sp soy sauce
4 tb-sp lard

1 bunch celery
1 t-p cornflour
½ t-sp salt

Remove the leaves and old parts of the celery and cut the rest into 1½ inch sections and then into shreds. Cut the meat into similar shape but rather smaller and mix with cornflour, a little water and soy sauce. Heat 2 tb-sp lard and fry the meat shreds. It will be better to fry the fat part first if there is any. Stir on a brisk fire for 2 minutes. Heat the remaining lard and fry the celery for 2 minutes. Add the meat shreds with salt. Mix thoroughly and stir for 2 minutes more and serve.

冬 筍 炒 肉 絲
Fried Pork Shreds With Bamboo Shoots

1 lb. bamboo shoots
½ lb. pork
1 egg
2—3 spring onions
2 tb-sp soy sauce

½ t-sp salt
4 tb-sp cooking oil
½ t-sp sugar
1 t-sp cornflour

Remove the outer skin of the bamboo shoots and cut off ½ inch from the roots which should be thrown away. Shred both the bamboo shoots and pork. Then cut the spring onions into sections. Mix the pork with soy sauce, egg, cornflour and sugar.

Heat 2 tb-sp cooking oil till hot and fry the pork shreds for 2 minutes. Remove from fire. Heat the remaining oil and fry the bamboo shoots with ½ t-sp salt. Keep on stirring for 3 minutes. Pour in the cooked pork and sectioned spring onions. Stir again for ½ minute and serve.

Meat

四 季 豆 炒 肉 片
Fried Slices Pork With French Beans

½ lb. pork (lean)   1 tb-sp soy sauce
½ lb. French beans   4 tb-sp lard
1 t-sp cornflour   ½ t-sp salt

Cut the meat into thin oblong slices and mix with thin cornflour paste. Cut the beans into ½ inch sections and fry in 2 tb-sp lard and ½ t-sp salt for 3 minutes; add 1 tb-sp water if it tends to dry. Remove from fire. Heat the rest of the lard and fry the meat for 5 minutes with soy sauce. Mix in the already fried beans and serve.

Variation : ½ lb. green peas.

綠 豆 芽 炒 肉 絲
Fried Pork Shreds With Pea Sprouts

½ lb. pea sprouts   1 tb-sp soy sauce
6 ozs. pork   2 tb-sp lard
1 t-sp salt

Remove the heads and ends of the pea sprouts. Wash them clean and put them in boiling water for 5 minutes. Drain away the water and soak the pea sprouts in cold boiled water.

Cut the meat into shreds. Heat the lard and fry the pork shreds on a big fire with soy sauce and salt for 3 minutes. Remove from fire, mix the pea sprouts which have been drained again.

It is not advisable to fry the pea sprouts too long. Soak them in boiling water to produce crispness which is absent if they are fried. Pea sprouts can be eaten raw if properly washed.

煎 肉 片
Fried Pork Tenderloin

1 lb. pork tenderloin   2 cups soup
3/4 cup sherry   1 t-sp sesame oil or olive oil
4 tb-sp cooking oil or lard   1 bud garlic
                                  1 t-sp rice flour
¼ cup soy sauce   1 t-sp aniseed powder
1 t-sp sugar   ¼ lb. ham

Cut the pork tenderloin into strips about an inch in size. Place the meat in a deep bowl, pour the wine over and stir occasionally for 15 minutes. Wash in cold water and dry between the folds of a clean piece of cloth.

Meat

Bring the lard to boiling point in a frying pan and add the pork strips, stirring constantly with a pair of chopsticks. When turned a light brown, put the soup stock, soy sauce and ham, aniseed powder and crushed garlic. Do not cover the pan. When the liquid has been reduced ⅓, add sugar. Now put in the rice flour, and when the mixture begins to thicken, quickly add the small amount of olive oil or sesame oil. This recipe calls for a very quick fire, otherwise the meat is inclined to toughen.

This is an ideal dish when served with rice. These two will make a complete meal. When prepared by an expert Chinese chef, it is most difficult to distinguish between pork and chicken.

紅 燒 糯 米 猪 肚
Braised Tripe With Glutinous Rice

1 tripe	2 oz. minced ham
5 eggs	4 oz. glutinous rice
1 t-sp salt	½ cup soy sauce
2 spring onions	1 tb-sp sherry (optional)

Wash the tripe carefully with salt or starch and be sure that there is no smell. Spend more time in washing the inside of the tripe than outside. Use a piece of string to tie up one side of the tripe. Wash the rice and beat the eggs, then mix them together with soy sauce, sherry and ham. Put the mixture into the tripe. Tie up the other end of the tripe put it in a heavy pot with 2 cups of water. As soon as it boils, add the sherry and mix in the salt after 1½ hours later. Cook for another 1 hour, cut into slices or strips. Arrange on a plate and serve.

紅 燒 猪 肚
Braised Tripe

1 tripe	2 tb-sp lard or cooking oil
12 fresh mushrooms	2 tb-sp soy sauce
½ t-sp salt	2 onions

Wash the tripe with salt and starch very carefully as in the preceding recipe. Boil it with 1 pint of water on a very low fire for 2 hours. Cut the tripe into strips. Fry lightly for a minute in the lard or cooking oil with the shredded onions and salt. Add half a pint of water, 2 tb-sp soy sauce and mushrooms, then simmer for ½ hour.

Meat

冬 筍 炒 豬 腰

Fried Kidney With Bamboo Shoots

1 pair kidneys	½ t-sp salt
½ lb. bamboo shoots	1 t-sp vinegar
4 tb-sp soy sauce	1 tb-sp cornflour
2 tb-sp wine	½ t-sp sugar

Cut kidneys into two halves and remove all the white gristle. Cut about 1/10 inch deep crosswise and then into 1 inch slices. Soak them in water first for a few minutes and then into the wine before using.

Cut the bamboo shoots into thin slices. Heat 1 tb-sp lard and fry the bamboo shoots with salt for 3 minutes. Remove from fire. Then heat the remaining lard till smoking and fry the kidney for 3 minutes. Add in the soy sauce, sugar, vinegar and cornflour with ½ cup of water. Heat until the gravy is translucent and serve.

The kidneys should not be fried too long as they will become tough and shrink in size.

菜 花 炒 豬 腰

Fried Kidney With Cauliflower

1 pair kidneys	1 tb-sp soy sauce
1 tb-sp sherry	½ lb. cauliflower
1 t-sp cornflour	4 tb-sp lard
3—4 slices ginger and spring onion	½ t-sp salt

Remove gristle of the kidneys and cut them into about 1 inch pieces. On top of each piece make some slashes crosswise. Soak them in water and then in sherry before cooking. Mix well with the cornflour, 1 tb-sp water and soy sauce. Cut the cauliflower into pieces. Heat 2 tb-sp lard and fry the cauliflower with ¼ t-sp salt for 5 minutes. Remove from pan. Again heat the remaining lard, take the kidneys out from sherry and fry them. In order to make them tender it is very important to fry on a very high fire and stir well for 3 minutes. Add the cooked cauliflower, sherry, soy sauce, cornflour, sliced ginger and sectioned spring onion. Mix them well in the pan and stir for 1 minute more. Serve immediately.

Meat

炒　猪　肝
Fried Liver

1 lb. liver	1 t-sp cornflour
1 oz. spring onion	3 tb-sp lard
½ t-sp salt	1 tb-sp sherry (optional)
2 tb-sp soy sauce	1 t-sp sugar

Wash and cut the spring onions into 1 inch sections. Cut the liver into thin slices and mix with cornflour, sherry, sugar, ginger and soy sauce. Heat the lard nad fry on a very strong heat and add the sectioned spring onions. Keep stirring until each piece turns pale brown, then pour in the salt and stir for ½ minute and serve.

牛　肉
Beef

Beef is not so commonly eaten as pork in China and is harder to cook. Some people do not like the smell of beef and have never tried to like it with the result that some have not tasted it during their life time. Beef is the principal meal of Mohammedans, but non-Mohammedans think beef is not so tasty. Since the demand for beef is low the price of beef in the market in China is also low.

Different parts of beef are needed for different kinds of dishes. For frying, tenderloin or sirloin is best; for braising, shin or shank is good and for stewing, of course, stew beef is suitable. Beef is tougher than pork. For braising a longer time is taken, about ½ hour more, and the braised beef should be cut 1 to 1½ inches in squares against the grain. A shorter times, however, must be used if beef is fried. As soon as the fried beef is in the frying pan, it must be stirred constantly on a good brisk fire for not more than 2 minutes, if longer than that the meat will become tough and hard to masticate. Always cut the beef into thin slices against the grain for frying, and any part of the fat or muscle which seems to be tough should be thrown away.

In a Chinese restaurant, the chef always heats ½ lb. or 1 lb. lard till smoking. The quantity of oil used depends on the amount of meat. In this oil, the seasoned beef ought to be fried for 1 minute. Then he removes it from the fire and drains the oil, then mixes it with the already fried vegetables, sauce or any other ingredients. Beef cooked in this way,

Meat

of course, will be more tender and tasty, besides, it can hardly be distinguished from fried pork. However, the Chinese housewives who are always thrifty and economical do not like to consume a liberal amount of oil, as used by the restaurant chef who can use the remaining oil for other dishes. Chinese housewives use only a little oil and fry the beef on a brisk fire very fast

Beef balls, no matter how cleverly they can be prepared, can never be as good as pork balls.

紅 燒 整 塊 牛 肉
Braised Beef (Whole)

2 lbs. beef-shin or shank	3—4 slices ginger
1 cup soy sauce	3—4 spring onions
1 cup sherry	1 piece star aniseed or
1 t-sp sugar	½ t-sp cinnamon

Wash the beef and put it in a heavy pot with soy sauce. Bring it to boiling point, add sherry, ginger, spring onion and 2 bowls of water. Cover the pot tightly and cook over a very low fire for 3 hours. Add the sugar and simmer another ½ hour. When it becomes cold cut into thin slices and arrange on a serving plate; pour the gravy on the top of the sliced beef and serve.

Same method and ingredients are used for braised liver and tongue, put them into the same pot and braise them only increasing the seasoning proportionally.

紅 燒 牛 肉
Braised Beef (In Pieces)

2 lbs. beef-shin or shank	½ tb-sp sugar
1 cup soy sauce	3—4 slices ginger
½ cup sherry (optional)	2—3 spring onions

Cut the meat into 1½ inch squares and put them into a heavy pot with soy sauce. Bring it to boil, add sherry, ginger, spring onion and 2 bowls water. Simmer on a low fire for 2 hours. Then add sugar and again cook for ½ hour more and serve.

紅 燒 葫 蘿 菠 牛 肉
Braised Beef With Carrots And Potatoes

2 lbs. stewing beef	1½ cups soy sauce
8 carrots	1 slice ginger
½ lb. celery	4 onions
4 potatoes	1 spring onion

Meat

Cut the beef into 1 inch or 1½ squares and place them in a bowl, covering them with cold water twice the depth of the beef. Soak for 1 hour or more. Drain the meat and place it in a boiler with double the amount of boiling water. Add 1¼ cup of soy sauce, sectioned spring onions, sliced ginger and simmer over a slow fire about 2½ hours until the beef is thoroughly done. Remove the beef from pot, cover with enough gravy to keep moist, and place in a warm oven.

Place the quartered carrots, onions, potatoes and section celery in the remaining gravy with the remaining ¼ cup soy sauce. Cover and cook for about 20 minutes, or until vegetables are done. Place the vegetables around the cooked beef, add sufficient gravy and serve.

It may be served with either rice, noodles or pastry.

紅 燒 蕃 茄 牛 肚
Braised Beef Tripe With Tomato And Onion

1 lb. beef tripe
½ cup soy sauce
¼ lb. onion
¼ lb. tomato
1 t-sp sugar
½ t-sp salt

Wash the tripe very thoroughly with salt. Put the whole piece of tripe in a pot and add 3 cups water. Start with low fire after boiling and simmer for 3 hours then take it out and cut the tripe about ½ inch wide by 1½ inches long. Put the tripe back into the pot.

Cut each onion and tomato into 4 sections and put them in the pot to simmer with the soy sauce and salt. Continue to simmer for another hour then add the sugar. Cook about 10 more minutes and serve.

紅 燒 蕃 茄 牛 肉
Braised Beef With Tomato And Onion

1 lb. beef (lean)
4 tomatoes
2 onions
½ cup soy sauce
½ t-sp sugar

Wash the beef, cut into 1 or 1½ inch squares. Cut each tomato and onion into quarters. Put the beef and 2 cups of water in a heavy pot on a big fire. When it starts to boil, add the soy sauce and ginger. Cover the pot tight and put on a very low fire and cook for 2 hours. Then add the tomatoes and onions and cook for ½ hour longer. Add sugar and cook about 10 minutes before serving.

Meat

紅 燒 牛 舌
Braised Ox Tongue

1 tongue (2 — 3 lbs.)
1 cup soy sauce
8 tb-sp sherry (optional)
1 t-sp salt

1 t-sp sugar
2 spring onions
2 — 3 slices ginger

Put enough water in a heavy pot to cover the tongue and boil for 5 minutes in boiling water. Take it out and pour off the water. Remove the outer white skin of the tongue. Put it back into the pot and pour in the soy sauce, sherry, ginger, spring onion and 2 bowls of water. Cook under a low fire for 1½ hours, add sugar and cook for another 15 minutes.

Slice into pieces when it is cold. Heat the gravy and pour it on the top of the sliced tongue and serve.

This dish is also very good if put in the refrigerator till the juice is frozen into jelly. Take it out with its jelly and cut into slices and serve.

燻 牛 肉 片
Smoked Slices Beef

2 lb. beef
½ cup soy sauce
1 tb-sp salt
1 tb-sp aniseed powder

3 tb-sp brown sugar
3 — 4 slices ginger
2 — 3 spring onions

Cut the beef in thin but big slices. Put all ingredients and 1½ cups of water in the pot. Then heat on a low fire after boiling. Simmer continuously for 1½ hours. Put the aniseed powder and brown sugar in a pan and arrange the beef on the top of the iron grate. Then place the grate over the pan and cover the lid. Heat on fire until the smoke makes the meat brown and serve.

燻 牛 肉 丸
Smoked Beef Balls

2 lbs. beef
2 tb-sp soy sauce
2 t-sp salt
1 cup cornflour

1 tb-sp sesame oil
1 tb-sp chopped spring onion
1 t-sp chopped ginger

Meat

Remove the muscle and fat of the beef then chop it very finely. Mix in the cornflour, sesame oil, salt and soy sauce, chopped spring onion ginger and 2 tb-sp of water. Make them into 15 balls and boil them in boiling water for about ½ minute. Arrange them on the smoking grate and smoke in the same way as the above recipe and serve.

牛 肉 丸

Beef Balls

1 lb. lean beef	½ lb. spinach or cabbage
¼ cup breadcrumbs	1 egg
¼ cup flour	Few slices ginger
½ t-sp salt	½ t-sp sugar
¼ cup soy sauce	½ lb. cooking oil

The beef should be lean without any muscle or fat. Mince or chop the beef and mix well with bread crumbs and egg. Add a little flour and ¼ cup of water. Make into 8 balls. Then heat the oil till smoking, and fry light brown. Drain the oil and simmer in ½ cup water and ¼ cup of sauce on a very low fire for ½ hour. Wash the cabbage or spinach and cut them as desired. Heat 1 tb-sp oil and fry the vegetable with ½ t-sp salt and stir for 1 minute. Add the meat balls and simmer with spinach for 3 minutes. If cabbage is used simmer for 20 minutes.

葱 頭 炒 牛 肉

Fried Beef Slices With Onion

½ lb. beef	1 tb-sp sherry (optional)
½ lb. onions	½ t-sp sugar
2 tb-sp soy sauce	4 tb-sp lard
1 tb-sp cornflour	½ t-sp salt
1 egg	

Cut the beef against the grain into slices. Mix with cornflour with 1 tb-sp water, soy sauce, sherry, egg and sugar. Cut onions into ½ inch thick slices. Heat 1 tb-sp lard and fry the onions with salt for 3 minutes and then take them out from pan. Heat the remaining lard till smoking and put in the seasoned beef and stir constantly on a brisk fire for 1 minute. Add the onion and stir for 1 minute and serve with pepper.

Meat

青 椒 炒 牛 肉
Fried Beef With Green Pepper

½ lb. beef tenderloin
4 oz. green pepper
1 tb-sp cornflour
1 egg
1 tb-sp sherry (optional)

½ t-sp sugar
6 tb-sp lard or vegetable oil
½ t-sp salt
1 t-sp tomato sauce
2 tb-sp soy sauce

Cut the tenderloin into thin slices. Wash the pepper and cut into rather bigger slices than the beef. Mix the sliced beef with soy sauce, sherry, egg, cornflour, sugar, and tomato sauce. Fry the pepper with 2 tb-sp of oil and ½ t-sp salt for 3 minutes and remove from fire. Let the rest of the oil spread over the whole frying pan, and fry the sliced beef on a very big fire for 1 minute, in order to prevent sticking to the frying pan. Stir quickly and constantly. Add the already fried pepper and stir another minute and serve.

炒 牛 肝
Fried Beef Liver

½ lb. liver
½ lb. spring onions
1 tb-sp cornflour
6 tb-sp lard

2 tb-sp soy sauce
½ tb-sp sherry
2—3 slices ginger
½ t-sp salt

Cut the liver into slices. Season with soy sauce, salt, sherry and sugar. Mix in the cornflour and 1 tb-sp water. Cut the spring onions into sections. Heat the lard till hot and fry the liver for 3 minutes, add in the sectioned spring onion and stir for ½ minute. When the liver turns pale, serve with pepper and eat while hot.

冬 菰 炒 牛 肉
Fried Beef Slices And Mushrooms

½ lb. beef
10 mushrooms
½ t-sp salt
1 tb-sp sherry (optional)
6 tb-sp lard

2 tb-sp soy sauce
3—4 slices ginger
1 tb-sp cornflour
1 egg
½ t-sp sugar

Meat

Choose medium size mushrooms and cut off the stems and wash them. Soak in ½ cup of hot water before using. Cut the beef against the grain into very thin slices. Mix with soy sauce, sugar, sherry, chopped ginger, egg, and cornflour. Heat 2 tb-sp lard and fry the mushroom with salt for 2 minutes, pour in the water in which they were soaked and simmer for 5 minutes then remove from the fire.

Heat the remaining lard on a good big fire and fry the seasoned beef. Stir fast and constantly for 1 minute. Add in the cooked mushroom and stir until it boils. Arrange the mushroom with the black side up on the top of the beef and serve piping hot.

芹菜炒牛肉
Fried Beef With Celery

½ lb. beef tenderloin	½ t-sp sugar
4 oz. celery	6 tb-sp lard
2 tb-sp soy sauce	½ t-sp salt
1 tb-sp cornflour	½ t-sp pepper
1 tb-sp sherry (optional)	1 egg

Cut the celery 1 inch in length and slice the beef against the grain very thin. Mix the sliced beef steak with soy sauce, egg, sherry, cornflour and sugar. Heat 2 tb-sp lard till hot and fry the celery with the salt for 3 minutes, then remove from fire. Heat the rest of the lard till smoking hot, and fry the sliced beef steak over a very brisk fire. In order to prevent sticking in the frying pan and to have tender beef, stir quickly and constantly for 1 minute when each piece of meat turns pale brown. Add the cooked celery and serve.

炒蠔油牛肉
Fried Beef In Oyster Sauce

1 lb. beef tenderloin	1 t-sp sugar
2 tb-sp oyster sauce	1 t-sp salt
½ tb-sp soy sauce	1 spring onion
1 egg	1 tb-sp sherry or
1 tb-sp cornflour	2 tb-sp water
6 tb-sp lard	

Cut the beef as usual and section the spring onion. Mix the beef with soy sauce, cornflour, egg, salt and spring onion thoroughly. Heat the lard till very hot, pour the seasoned beef into the pan and stir

Meat

constantly on a good brisk fire for 1 minute. Then add the oyster sauce and sugar. Cook and stir for half more minute. This dish should be served immediately after it is cooked.

炒蕃茄牛肉
Fried Beef With Tomato

1 lb. beef tenderloin	1 t-sp salt
2 tb-sp tomato sauce	6 tb-sp lard
1 tb-sp soy sauce	¼ lb. tomatoes
1 tb-sp sherry (optional)	3—4 slices ginger
1 tb-sp cornflour	

Cut the steak as usual and cut tomatoes into slices. Mix the beef with soy sauce, sherry, egg, ginger, and cornflour. Heat 2 tb-sp lard and fry the tomato first with the salt. Stir for 1 minute then remove from fire. Heat the remaining lard on a big fire till smoking, put in the seasoned beef and stir constantly for 1 minute. Then add tomato sauce and keep on stirring for half more minute. Mix in the cooked tomatoes and serve immediately.

蒸牛肉
Steamed Beef

1 lb. stewing beef	1 t-sp salt
20 mushrooms	1 tb-sp soy sauce
1 tb-sp sherry (optional)	1 spring onion

Cut the meat into 1½ inch squares and season with sherry, and soy sauce. Put in a deep basin or bowl and steam in a steamer with the lid on for 4 hours. Wash the mushrooms and cut off the stems. Add 1 cup of water, stir well and steam with beef for ½ hour after the water in the bowl starts to boil. It will be ready to serve when the gravy becomes brown. Serve with pepper and salt.

五香牛肉鬆
Spiced Beef Shreds

2 lbs. beef (lean)	2 cups chicken soup
¾ cup soy sauce	½ t-sp aniseed powder or cinnamon
¾ cup sherry (optional)	
8 tb-sp lard	

Meat

Put enough lard or about half of the above amount into a pan to prevent the beef from sticking. After removing all fat and tendons from the beef, place it in the pan. Then add the chicken soup, wine, and soy sauce and boil until the meat is tender and the liquid is gone.

When the meat cools, tear it into shreds or put through a grinder and grind very fine. Place the shreded beef back in the frying pan with the prevent the beef from sticking. After removing all fat and tendons from. Stir constantly while cooking. Remove to a clean container. The shreded beef will be able to keep for many days.

This extraordinary dish is sometimes served as an hors d'œuvre at a Chinese dinner. It is also used to sprinkle on top of plain boiled noodles, or to serve as an accompaniment of congee for breakfast. It is not difficult to prepare and it possesses the qualities for long keeping.

羊 肉
Mutton And Lamb

There are different kinds of mutton and lamb meat, but to the Chinese there is no difference. People from North China eat more of it. Owing to the peculiar odour of mutton, beef is more in demand. It is warm in nature somewhat like wine; so it is mostly eaten during winter.

Chinese doctors recommend mutton especially to invalids owing to its nutritious properties. It is easily digested. It is best cooked in brass pots.

紅 燒 羊 肉
Braised Mutton Or Lamb

1 lb. mutton or lamb	½ t-sp sugar
1 big turnip	1 t-sp salt
½ cup soy sauce	2—3 spring onions
½ cup sherry	

Select a fine piece of lamb or mutton. Cut into 1½ inch squares. Simmer in a pot with 3 cups of water on a low fire for half an hour. Take a turnip, pierce it with a meat skewer and place it in the centre of the meat cubes. Put it in the pot also and bring this to the boil. Skim the scum if any. Then remove the turnip from the fire and add the sherry and cook for another half an hour before adding the soy sauce and salt. Keep on cooking for 20 minutes then add sugar and spring onion about 5 minutes before serving. Serve piping hot in a large bowl, pouring over the sauce just before the time to eat

Meat

The use of turnip is recommended to absorb the peculiar smell of the mutton. The smell will be very strong if sherry is added to the pot while the turnip and mutton are stewing at the same time.

Lamb prepared in the above manner will be found most acceptable as a Chinese dinner course or as the mainstay of a foreign dinner.

橘 皮 燉 羊 肉
Stewed Mutton With Orange Peel

2 lbs. leg of mutton	2 t-sp salt
1 tb-sp sherry	1 slice ginger
1 oz. dried orange peel	

Cut the meat into fairly large pieces about 1½ inch squares, and place in a boiler with 4 cups of water. Bring to the boil then remove to a low fire and add the sherry, ginger and dried orange peel. Simmer for 2 hours, stir a few times during the process of cooking. Add salt and simmer for ½ hour longer before serving

凍 羊 膏
Cold Jellied Lamb Or Mutton

1 lb. lamb	1 tb-sp sherry
1 oz. spring onions	½ t-sp salt
2 tb-sp soy sauce	

Cut the mutton into pieces about 1½ inch squares. Put them in a heavy pot. Heat over big fire with two bowls of water until boiling. Add the chopped spring onions, soy sauce, salt and simmer on a low fire for 1½ hours. Put in a soup plate then in a refrigerator or a cool place overnight, then turn it into a flat dish and cut it up into squares of thick slices as desired. This dish can be kept in the refrigerator for 1 or 2 weeks. It is, therefore, all right to double or treble the recipe to make enough for future use as well. It is good to go with wine for those people who do not eat lamb or mutton in any other form, especially when they are not told beforehand.

People in Peiping are specialists in preparing this popular dish.

Meat

葱 頭 炒 羊 肉
Fried Lamb With Onions

1 lb. lamb or mutton
½ t-sp minced ginger
2 medium-sized onions

½ cup soy sauce
4 tb-sp lard

Slice the lamb or mutton into very thin slices. Heat the oil in a frying pan till smoking and add the lamb or mutton and ginger. Stir constantly until the meat is well seared. Add the sliced onions and soy sauce, bring to quick boil and serve while very hot.

This is a very appetising dish when eaten with rice and has the additional advantage of being very easy and quick to prepare.

韭 菜 黄 炒 羊 肉
Fried Lamb With Young Leeks

½ lb. lamb
½ lb. young leeks
6 spring onions
1 t-sp minced ginger

4 tb-sp lard
2 tb-sp soy sauce
½ t-sp salt

The meat should first be diced quite fine, the vegetables and onion being shredded into thin strips not over 1½ inches in length. Fry the diced meat, ginger and shredded onion with soy sauce for about 2 minutes over a brisk fire in hot oil. Then add the vegetable, salt and some water and cook for one more minute.

The time of cooking will depend upon what vegetable is used. Cabbage, spring onion, leeks, spinach, celery, french-beans or almost any green vegetable desired can be substituted in this recipe. The dish is usually served alone or with other similar dishes when rice forms the basis of the meal.

粉 條 炒 羊 肉
Fried Lamb With Chinese Vermicelli

½ lb. lamb
¼ lb. vermicelli
  (peastarch noddles)
3—4 spring onions
½ t-sp salt

1—2 slices ginger
1 tb-sp sherry (optional)
4 tb-sp lard or cooking oil
1 tb-sp soy sauce

Meat

Cut the meat into fine shreds and mix in thin cornflour paste and soy sauce. Soak the vermicelli in hot water for 5 minutes before using. Heat the lard in a frying pan and fry the meat quickly for 2 minutes, then add the vermicelli and mix well together. Add sherry, sectioned spring onions and salt. Fry quickly for another 2 minutes and pour in ¼ cup of water. Continue to fry for another two minutes more and serve.

炒 羊 肉 片
Fried Lamb Slices

1 lb. lamb	2 spring onions
2 tb-sp soy sauce	4 tb-sp lard
½ t-sp salt	1 tb-sp sherry (optional)
1 tb-sp cornflour	½ t-sp sugar

The most suitable cuts for dish are lamb tenderloin and the inside meat of lamb leg. Cut the meat into thin slices and mix with soy sauce, sherry, salt, sugar, cornflour and spring onion.

Heat the lard in a frying pan over a big fire until smoking, then put in the seasoned lamb slices and stir constantly for about 2 minutes add ¼ cup of water if necessary. Serve at once after it is cooked.

野 味

Chapter 5. Game

Wild game do not enter into the Chinese culinary art to any great extent, primarily because the flesh of wild animals and fowls is fibrous and therefore thought unpalatable. Wild duck, pheasant and pigeon are exceptions to the rule, however, and the following recipes ensure tender, savoury dishes which are most appetizing.

炒 野 鴨

Fried Wild Duck

1 wild duck
1 cup bean curd
½ cup lard
2 tb-sp sherry (optional)
1 t-sp salt
1 t-sp sugar
½ cup soy sauce
1 spring onion
½ t-sp aniseed powder
2 t-sp sesame oil or olive oil
2 cups stock

Place the lard in a deep pan and heat until piping hot, then add the duck which has previously been chopped with a sharp cleaver into 1 inch squares. It is essential that a sharp cleaver be used in order not to splinter the bones. Add the chopped spring onion, aniseed powder and fry them, stirring constantly over a low fire for half an hour. Now add the wine and cover the pan tightly and simmer for another ½ hour. Put in stock or water, soy sauce, diced bean curd and salt, and bring to the boil for about 10 minutes. Just before removing from the fire add the sugar and sesame oil and serve immediately.

紅 燒 五 香 野 鴨

Braised Spiced Wild Duck

1 wild duck
1 oz. spring onions
1 t-sp aniseed powder
3 tb-sp soy sauce
1 t-sp salt

Singe and draw the duck. Wash and drain well. Rub the inside with aniseed powder, insert the spring onions and pour in 1 tb-sp of soy sauce. Put the whole duck in a boiler and boil with 2 cups of water, salt and the remaining soy sauce. Test the meat with a fork. When it is done cut into pieces and serve.

The spring onions inside the duck can be used to fry with bean curds.

Game

鹹 野 雞

Salted Pheasant

1 pheasant
2 tb-sp salt
1 cup sherry (optional)
1 tb-sp Szechwan pepper or cinnamon

Remove the entrails well from the fresh pheasant but leave it unplucked. If Szechwan pepper is used, heat it with the salt in a hot frying pan and mix them well, wait until they are cold. Season the inside of the pheasant with the salt and pepper and damp it with cooking sherry. Hang the bird in a cold and airy place for a week or two, then pluck and singe well. Steam it on a low heat for 1 hour and cut as desired.

In case cinnamon is used it is not necessary to heat the cinnamon with the salt. Just mix them together and rub the inside of the pheasant.

炒 野 雞 丁

Fried Pheasant

1 pheasant breast and legs
½ t-sp salt
10 mushrooms
1 tb-sp sherry (optional)
1 tb-sp soy sauce
1 t-sp sugar
3 tb-sp lard

Cut the pheasant breast and the legs to about the size of grapes. Heat the lard till hot and fry the diced pheasant for about 5 minutes. Add the diced mushrooms and also the salt, soy sauce and a little water to prevent the ingredients becoming too dry. Stir for another 5 minutes. Add sugar, mix well and serve.

紅 燒 白 鴿

Braised Pigeon

4 pigeons
4 tb-sp soy sauce
2—3 spring onions
2—3 slices ginger

Singe and wash the pigeons. Draw them from the back of the tail and leave them as whole ones. Braise with 4 tb-sp soy sauce and 1 bowl of water. spring onion and ginger for 20 minutes under a low fire after the water starts to boil. During the process of cooking turn frequently so that every part of the bird is braised. When they are firm and cold cut them into pieces and lay the neck and bones on the bottom of the plate as foundation. It is a good cold dish to go with wine.

炸 五 香 白 鴿

Deep-Fried Spiced Pigeon

1 pigeon	2 t-sp salt
2 tb-sp honey	1 tb-sp sherry (optional)
½ lb. cooking oil	1 tb-sp aniseed powder

Kill and dress the pigeon as usual. Rub inside with salt and aniseed powder and the outside with honey. Heat the cooking oil till smoking then fry the pigeon until brown. Drain well and tear the pigeon into pieces and serve with pepper. This recipe should be doubled or tripled according to the number of diners.

炒 五 香 白 鴿

Fried Spiced Dove

2 doves	1 piece star aniseed
1 spring onion	4 oz. cabbage stakes
2—3 slices ginger	3 tb-sp lard
10 mushrooms	2 tb-sp soy sauce
2 cups sherry (optional)	½ t-sp salt

Kill and dress the doves. Cut only the breasts into thin slices. Heat the lard till hot and fry the sliced dove with ginger, spring onions, aniseed and salt. Add 1 cup of sherry and stir for a while. Cover the lid and add again 1 cup of chicken soup, soy sauce, cabbage stakes and mushroom. Cook for 5 minutes then add sugar. Stir well and serve.

Sea Food

海 味

Chapter 6. Sea Food

Sea food is only obtainable along the coastal provinces of China. The most typical sea food available are canned or dried abalone, dried razor clams, dried scallops and dried squids which are more savoury than the corresponding fresh ones if properly prepared. Dried scallops are widely used in making soup.

When shell fish are purchased be sure that they are fresh and their shells are tightly closed. Never pick those which gape and seem so weak that they can hardly close their shells as if they are drying. Care must be taken to eat the oysters raw, as Chinese consider them very nutritious when eaten raw.

Sea crabs can never be as good as fresh water crabs, but of course they can be prepared in the same way as fresh water crabs. When we talk about "Sea Flavour" we think of shark's fins.

Shrimps, prawns and lobsters belong to the same family. Fresh water shrimps and prawns are much better than sea-water shrimps and prawns.

蟹 鬆

Crab Shreds

2 lbs. crabs
2 tb-sp lard
4 tb-sp sherry (optional)
4 tb-sp soy sauce

1 t-sp sugar
5—6 slices ginger
2—3 spring onions

Wash the crabs and split them into two halves. Steam them with ginger and sherry. Take out the meat from the shell and legs. Heat the lard and fry the flesh on a low fire till the moisture is evaporated then add in soy sauce, sugar and fry them together until there is no more gravy. To cook this dish keep the fire very low and uniform in temperature throughout the period of cooking otherwise, the ingredients will be easily burnt.

Sea Food

蟹 蒸 蛋
Steamed Eggs With Crab

1 crab
2 eggs
2 oz. sherry
4 tb-sp soy sauce

½ oz. scallops
1 spring onion
1 t-sp lard

Steam the crab after it has been washed thoroughly clean. Remove the shell and take out the meat. Beat the eggs, mix with soy sauce and chopped spring onion. Wash the scallops and soak in the sherry. Then take them out and tear into shreds. Pour in the crab meat, scallop shreds, ½ cup of the water and the sherry in which the scallops were soaked into the beaten eggs. Mix them well with a pair of chopsticks. Put in the lard and steam for 15 minutes with lid tightly on. When the ingredients form a kind of consistency like custard the dish is done.

炒 蟹 肉
Fried Crab Meat

3 crabs
3 tb-s lard
¼ lb. pork
2 tb-sp soy sauce

1 tb-sp sherry (optional)
2 eggs
2 spring onions
½ t-sp salt

Wash the crabs and steam them. Remove the flesh from the shell and from the claws. Cut the pork into shreds, chop the spring onions and beat the eggs. Heat the lard and pour the eggs into the skillet and stir fast. Before the eggs are cooked, add in the crab meat and meat shreds, then mix them well. Add the soy sauce, sugar, salt and 2 tb-sp water. After 3 minutes mix the chopped spring onions and serve.

干 貝 炒 蛋
Scallop With Eggs

10 scallops
4 eggs
2 tb-sp lard

4 tb-sp sherry
1 t-sp salt

Soak the scallops in sherry over night and steam for ½ hour. Beat eggs; and add the already soften scallops and salt. Mix them thoroughly. Heat the lard till hot; pour the mixture and stir fast on a brisk fire for 2 minutes.

Sea Food

干 貝 鬆
Scallop Shreds

4 ozs. scallops	4 tb-sp sherry
4 tb-sp soy sauce	2 tb-sp lard

Soak the scallops in the sherry for 2 hours and boil with a cup of water. When they become soft; add the soy sauce and boil until the gravy is dry. Tear them into shreds. Heat the lard and let it spread all over the frying pan; put back the scallop shreds and keep on stirring on a low fire until all the moisture has evaporated. This dish can be kept very long and is a good accompanying dish for congee.

炒 海 參
Fried Sea Slugs

3 ozs. sea slugs	1 t-sp salt
3 ozs. bamboo shoots	1 t-sp sugar
½ lb. lean pork	1 spring onion
6 tb-sp lard	4 tb-sp soy sauce
½ cup sherry (optional)	

Brush away the sand from the sea slugs and heat them on the fire for few minutes. Soak them in water for 4 hours. Cut both the sea slugs and bamboo shoots into shreds and also the pork. Heat the lard till hot then fry the sea slugs and meat shreds. Stir constantly while frying. Pour in the wine, soy sauce, salt, bamboo shoots and ½ cup of water. Boil for 15 minutes and add sugar and sectioned spring onion.

青 蒸 哈 唎
Steamed Clams

1 bowl clams	1 t-sp chopped ginger
¾ cup sherry (optional)	1 t-sp sesame oil
½ cup soy sauce	

Wash the clams clean and put them in a bowl with soy sauce and sherry; then steam for 5 — 10 minutes until the bivalves open. Season with chopped ginger and sesame oil.

This is a good accompanying dish for wine. Clams are rich in vitamins, minerals, calcium and starch.

Sea Food

Razor clams belong to the same family and the method of preparing is the same. Remove the white fibre in the clam while eating because it is too cold to be eaten from the Chinese point of view.

炒 鮑 魚 片

Fried Abalone

1 can abalone	1 t-sp salt
¼ lb. mushrooms	4 tb-sp lard
½ lb. bamboo shoots	2 spring onions

Cut the bamboo shoots into thin slices and wash the mushrooms which should be soaked in hot water before using. Again slice the abalone. Heat the lard and fry the mushrooms and bamboo shoots with 1 t-sp salt and stir constantly. Then add the mushroom water and cook over a medium fire for 5 minutes. Put in the sliced abalone and sectioned spring onion and stir for 1 minute and serve.

炒 魷 魚

Fried Squids

1 lb. squid	1 tb-sp soy sauce
4 tb-sp lard	1 tb-sp sherry (optional)
1 spring onion	1 tb-sp cornflour
½ t-sp salt	2–3 slices ginger

Select the small squids. Pull out the centre bones of the squids and wash off the skin. Clean inside thoroughly. Cut off and keep the tentacles for frying. Slit open and then cut into 1½ inch squares. Again cut a few slashes lengthwise and crosswise on each square piece.

Cut the spring onions into sections. Heat the lard over a big fire till hot. Then put in the squids, the spring onions and ginger and stir for 1 minute. Then add the salt, soy sauce and sherry. Stir again for 2 minutes. Mix the cornflour with 2 tb-sp water and pour it into the skillet and cook until it becomes translucent. Serve promptly after cooking.

Sea Food

油 浸 海 蜇

Oiled-Fried Sea Blubber

2 pieces sea blubber
4 tb-sp soy sauce
3 tb-sp cooking oil

1 spring onion
1 t-sp sugar
1 t-sp sesame oil or olive oil

Wash the sea blubber with lukewarm water. Place in a big bowl and put the sugar and chopped ginger on top. Heat the oil till hot and pour the hot oil on the sea blubber. Mix well while pouring the oil. Add soy sauce and sesame oil and serve.

The hot oil will cause the sea blubber to contract in size.

海 蜇 拌 蘿 菠 絲

Sea Blubber Skin With Turnip Shreds

3 sea blubber skins
1 turnip
1 spring onion

4 tb-sp cooking oil
1 t-sp salt
1 t-sp sugar

Wash the sea blubber skins with hot water pull off the red stuff on the skin. Cut into fine shreds. Grate the turnip and mix in the salt. After ½ hour squeeze out the water and mix in the sugar, vinegar and chopped spring onion. Heat the oil till hot and pour on top of the grated turnip and shreded sea blubber skin and serve

冬 菰 炒 龍 蝦

Fried-Lobster Mushrooms

2 lbs. lobsters
6 tb-sp lard
3 tb-sp cornflour
2 tb-sp soy sauce
1 tb-sp sherry (optional)

¼ lb. mushrooms
1 bud garlic
3—4 slices ginger
½ t-sp salt

The lobsters can be either boiled or steamed. Boil the lobsters for 3 minutes or steam them in a steamer for 8 minutes. Remove the flesh from the shell and cut into neat shapes. Then dip lightly in thin cornflour

Sea Food

paste. Fry the mushrooms in 2 tb-sp lard with salt for 5 minutes and remove from fire. Fry the lobsters quickly on high fire in the remaining half of the lard for 3 minutes, then mix with the mushrooms and fry them together for another 3 minutes. Add garlic, ginger slices, sherry and soy sauce and mix them thoroughly for 1 minute and serve hot.

炸 龍 蝦
Deep-Fried Lobsters

2 lbs. fresh lobsters   1 t-sp salt
1 lb. cooking oil   3 tb-sp cornflour
1 egg

Clean the fresh lobsters and steam them as in the preceding recipe. Remove the flesh from the shells. Cut the lobster into small pieces and dip in a batter made of cornflour, egg, 3 tb-sp water and salt. Bring the cooking oil to the boil and drop the pieces of lobsters one by one into the oil and fry until a golden brown. Serve with pepper.

燴 龍 蝦
Lobsters With Meat Sauce

3 lobsters   1/4 lb. pork (minced)
2 eggs   2 tb-sp sherry (optional)
2 spring onions   2 tb-sp cornflour
2 tb-sp soy sauce   6 tb-sp lard
1 t-sp salt   2—3 slices ginger

There are two methods of cooking this dish: one is to steam the lobsters before they are fried and second is to fry them alive.

The first method. Chop or grind the pork chop. Steam the lobsters in a big steamer for 8 minutes; a longer time will be required if the lobsters are large in size. Cut each lobster lengthwise into parts, then across into 1½ inch sections with the shells on. Again chop each head into 4 parts and each claw into 3 sections. Beat the eggs and mix thoroughly with the chopped spring onion, ginger, soy sauce, salt, meat, sherry, cornflour and ½ cup of water.

The second method. Cut the raw lobsters into the same portions and take off the dark gritty stuff from the heads. Prepare all the ingredients as in the preceding method.

Heat the lard in a skillet over a big fire till hot. Put in the lobsters and stir for 7 minutes, then pour in the meat sauce and stir continuously over a big fire for 3 minutes. If the lobsters are large longer cooking time should be given.

Points to remember. Fresh boiled lobsters are always better than boiled ones bought from fishmongers. Steamed lobsters are usually more tender than those boiled. Lobsters fried alive are always more tasty than those steamed.

蒸 龍 蝦

Steamed Lobsters

3 lobsters
1 tb-sp (optional)
3—4 slices ginger

1 spring onion
2 tb-sp soy sauce

Cut each lobster lengthwise into two and remove the dark gritty stuff in the head. Place the lobsters with shells on the tier of a steamer with the shells underneath.

Chop the spring onions and ginger very finely and mix together with soy sauce, sherry and 2 tb-sp water. Put a little of it on each cut lobster. Cover steamer and steam over big fire for 15 minutes after the water starts to boil. A longer time may be required if the lobsters are large.

冬 筍 炒 蝦 仁

Fried Shelled Prawns With Bamboo Shoots

1 lb. prawns
6 t-sp lard
1 tb-sp soy sauce
1 t-sp salt

½ tb-sp sherry (optional)
4 oz. bamboo shoots
½ t-sp sugar
2 spring onions

Shell the prawns and remove the gritty stuff by cutting 1/16 inch of the back and pull them out. Wash them clean and drain the extra moisture. Soak in the sherry before cooking. Heat the lard till hot and fry the prawns for 2 minutes then add the sliced bamboo shoots and stir them together for 3 minutes. Season with salt and soy sauce. Add 1 tb-sp of water if necessary. Mix in the sugar and stir for ½ minute longer. Season with pepper and garnish with sectioned spring onion and serve.

Sea Food

炒 蝦

Fried Prawns With Shells

1 lb. prawns	½ t-sp salt
8 tb-sp cooking oil	2 tb-sp soy sauce
1 tb-sp sherry (optional)	1 t-sp vinegar
1 spring onion	1 t-sp sugar
1 t-sp chopped ginger	

Use a pair of scissors to trim off the whiskers and tails. Wash them clean and drain properly. Heat 6 tb-sp oil and fry the prawns for 5 minutes. Stir constantly while frying. Remove from fire and heat the remaining oil till smoking. Pour in again the prawns for second frying for 5 minutes, this makes the prawns brown and crisp. Stir constantly while frying. Season with salt, soy sauce, sherry, chopped ginger, sectioned spring onion, sugar and vinegar. Add 1 tb-sp of water if the gravy tends to become dry. Mix all the ingredients thoroughly for ½ minute and serve.

醉 蝦

Drunken Shrimps

1 lb. fresh live shrimps	2 tb-sp soy sauce
4 tb-sp sherry	1 t-sp salt
1 t-sp vinegar	1 t-sp chopped ginger

Select the best live shrimps and trim off the whiskers and tails with a pair of scissors. Wash them clean and rinse with cold boiled water. Put them in a bowl and pour in the sherry, salt and soy sauce. Cover with a saucer so that the shimps won't be able to jump out from the bowl after they are drunk. About 1 hour after, put them in a plate and mix with chopped ginger and vinegar. This is a good accompanying dish for wine.

The "Drunken Shrimps" is a famous dish of Hanchow in Chekiang Province. The shrimps are so-called because they are freshly pickled in liquor, soy sauce and ginger. For this recipe, fresh live shrimps must be used

Sea Food

油 炸 蝦
Oiled-Fried Prawns

1 lb. prawns
1 lb. cooking oil
4 t-sp soy sauce
1 t-sp salt
1 tb-sp sherry

Trim off whiskers and tails of the prawns and wash them thoroughly. Mix them with ½ t-sp salt and sherry. Put the soy sauce and remaining salt in a plate. Heat the oil till hot and place 2 tb-sp of oil in the soy sauce. Again fry the prawns in the oil until the colour turns red. Remove from fire and drain well. Put them on the plate which contains the soy sauce, salt and oil. Mix them thoroughly and serve.

炸 蝦 仁 麵 包
Shrimps On Toast

1 lb. shrimps
1 onion
1 t-sp salt
1 egg
1 t-sp flour
2 slices ginger
1 lb. cooking oil
Few slices of bread

Shell and wash the shrimps thoroughly. Mince the meat together with the onion, then add the flour and beaten egg. Cut the bread into thin slices and trim carefully. Divide each slice of bread into four portions. Put a small quantity of the shrimp paste on each piece.

Heat the cooking oil till smoking and fry the pieces until golden brown. Drain thoroughly and garnish with a bit of parsley or pepper according to taste. Serve hot.

炸 蝦 球
Fried Shrimp Balls

2 lbs. shrimps
½ lb. pork
2 tb-sp flour
1 t-sp sherry (opional)
1 egg
1 t-sp salt
2 tb-sp soy sauce
8 tb-sp cooking oil

Mince the pork and shrimps after they are washed and shelled thoroughly. Add beaten egg, flour, sherry, salt, and soy sauce to the ground pork and shrimps. Make the paste into pigeon-egg size balls.

Sea Food

Heat the oil till hot and fry both sides of the balls on a medium fire until they are light brown. Never use a big fire which will make them burn outside and leave them raw inside. Season with black pepper and salt according to taste and serve hot.

炒 蝦 仁
Fried Prawns

1 lb. fresh pawns	3—4 slices ginger
4 tb-sp cooking oil or lard	1 tb-sp soy sauce
	½ t-sp salt

Shell the prawns. Wash and clean carefully. Heat the oil in a frying pan till hot then add the prawns and the other ingredients in the order named. Fry for three to five minutes according to the size of the prawns.

冬 菰 炒 蝦 仁
Fried Prawns With Mushrooms

Use the same ingredients and add 10 big mushrooms and 2 extra tb-sp of lard. After washing and soaking the mushrooms in water about 10 minutes cut them into pieces about the same size as the shelled prawns, cook in the same way as the fried prawns. After frying mushrooms add an extra ½ t-sp salt. Stir constantly for 2 minutes.

青 豆 炒 蝦 仁
Fried Prawns With Green Peas

Use the same ingredients and add one small tin of green peas and two extra tb-sp of lard. Follow the same procedure as with fried prawns. After frying for 1 minute add the green peas and ½ t-sp salt and stir continuously for 2 minutes.

芙 蓉 蝦
Prawn *Fu-Yung*

1½ lbs. shrimps	3—4 slices ginger
1½ t-sp salt	8 eggs
1 tb-sp sherry (optional)	6 tb-sp lard

Sea Food

Shell and wash the prawns. Whip the eggs. Mix them up and add in all the seasoning. Heat the lard till hot and pour mixture into the frying pan. Stir over a good brisk fire for 2 to 3 minutes. Serve hot with pepper.

Use the same method and ingredients for crab *fu-yung*. Steam the crab first and take out the meat.

鳳 尾 蝦

Phoenix-Tail Prawns

1 lb. big prawns	1 tb-sp salt
1 egg	6 tb-sp lard
4 tb-sp flour	

Wash and shell the prawns but save the tails which turn a beautiful red during cooking and look like the tails of the phoenix. Open the back with a small knife just keep enough to let the black gritty stuff out. Whip the egg and mix with flour, salt and 2 tb-sp water. Put in the prawns which should be well coated with the mixture.

Heat the lard till hot and fry the prawns on both sides for about 3 minutes. Season with a little black pepper and salt to taste while serving.

蛋

Chapter 7. Egg

Eggs were considered very nutritious by the Chinese long before Western dietitians discovered their vitamin value. When the Chinese say eggs they always mean chicken eggs which are more commonly used than in Western countries. Duck eggs are not so popular and used only in making soups. Goose eggs are even less used.

To test an egg for freshness put the egg in a basin of water; if it floats the egg is not fresh.

肉 絲 蛋 包

Egg Omellet With Meat Shreds

8 eggs	6 tb-sp cooking oil
½ lb. meat shreds	2—3 spring onions
¼ lb. celery	½ t-sp sugar
¼ lb. pea sprouts	1 t-sp salt
2 tb-sp soy sauce	

Beat the eggs and mix in 1 t-sp salt. Cut the pork into shreds and cut the spring onion and celery across obliquely into shreds about 1 inch long. Wash the pea sprouts clean. Heat 2 tb-sp oil in a pan over a big fire. Put in the meat shreds and stir for 2 minutes. Pour the celery, pea sprouts and spring onion and stir constantly for 1 minute. Add in 2 tb-sp soy sauce and ½ t-sp sugar. Remove from fire after cooking for a while. Heat 4 more tb-sp oil till hot, turn on medium fire and pour in the well beaten eggs. Do not stir or break the mass. Leave it as it is but lift the bottom occasionally to make sure that it does not stick or burn. After 1 minute when the eggs are still partly in liquid form add in the meat, celery, spring onion and pea sprout on the top of the eggs. Do not pour in the juice which can be kept for further cooking. Fold one edge of the egg over the other.

If a little gravy is preferred heat the juice of the meat, celery, etc., and mix 1 tb-sp cornflour with 2 tb-sp water. Pour in the heated juice and heat till translucent. Again pour on top of the half folded egg and serve.

Egg

Variations:—
1. With shrimps ½ lb.
2. With chicken shreds ½ lb.
3. With oysters ½ lb.
4. With crab meat ½ lb.

蝦 仁 炒 蛋
Scrambled Eggs With Shrimps

8 eggs	4 tb-sp lard
½ lb. shrimps	1 t-sp salt
3 t-sp sherry (optional)	½ t-sp black pepper

Shell and wash the shrimps. Remove the black gritty stuff from the back; drain off all the extra moisture. With a pair of chopsticks or an egg beater beat the eggs thoroughly. Add salt, pepper and wine to the eggs and beat again. Mix in the shrimps. Heat the lard in a frying pan and pour in the mixture. Stir for 2 or 3 minutes or until the shrimps change colour.

火 腿 蒸 蛋
Steamed Ham And Egg

4 eggs	1 t-sp salt
¼ lb. ham	1 tb-sp lard

Beat the eggs and mince or chop the ham. Place them in a basin or bowl with 1 t-sp salt, 1 tb-sp lard and ½ cup of water. Mix well and place the bowl in a steamer or a boiler and steam for 15 minutes with lid on tightly. When it reaches the consistency of custard it is ready for serving.

火 腿 炒 蛋
Fried Ham And Egg

8 eggs	4 tb-sp lard
¼ lb. ham	1 t-sp salt

Mix the chopped ham with the well beaten eggs. Add the salt to the mixture and stir well. Heat the lard in a frying pan till hot, pour the ham and eggs into it and stir fast for 2 minutes. Season with pepper and serve.

燉 豬 肚 蛋
Simmered Tripe With Eggs

1 tripe	4 tb-sp soy sauce
20 eggs	1 tb-sp sesame oil
2 tb-sp sherry (optional)	1 t-sp salt

Wash the tripe with salt. Special attention should be paid in washing the inside of the tripe. After it is well cleaned, tie up one end with a piece of string break the eggs and add salt then pour into the tripe. Again tie the other end also and put in a heavy pot with 2 cups of water and soy sauce, salt and simmer on a low fire for 1½ hours after it starts to boil. Add the sherry and continue to simmer for another ½ hour. The fire should be just strong enough to keep the water boilding, otherwise, the water will dry up very quickly. Test with a fork to see if it is done. Cut into pieces and arrange on a plate; pour the soy sauce and sesame oil on top and serve either cold or hot.

紅 燒 雞 蛋
Braised Pork And Eggs

8 eggs	½ t-sp sugar
1 lb. pork	½ cup soy sauce
1 t-sp salt	

The pork selected should be fairly fat. Boil the eggs first for 5 minutes after the water starts to boil. Take them out and soak in cold water. Cut the pork into 1 inch squares; simmer in a heavy pot on a low fire with soy sauce, 2 cups of water and salt for 1½ hours. Shell the eggs, add in the pork and simmer them together for another ½ hour.

After the eggs are boiled and before they are braised they must be soaked in cold water otherwise the yolk will be tough and the shells cannot easily be removed when hot.

炸 火 腿 雞 蛋 丸
Fried Ham Balls With Eggs

1 lb. ham (lean)	6 slices of bread
6 eggs	1 lb. cooking oil
1 t-sp flour	½ t-sp salt

Egg

Cook the ham and put it through a grinder, or preferably, mince very fine with a sharp cleaver. Beat the eggs thoroughly and add in the ham and sufficient shreded bread—all the crust of the bread should be removed. Then add enough flour to make a thick paste. Roll the mixture in the palms to make small balls the size of chestnuts. Heat the cooking oil till smoking and fry the ham balls until a golden brown.

There is no need to season the ham with too much salt if Chinese ham is used because it is always salty enough, otherwise one more t-sp of salt should be added to the mixture before frying.

蛋 餃

Egg Dumplings

6 eggs	1 t-sp salt
½ lb. pork	2—3 spring onions
3 t-sp soy sauce	2—3 slices ginger
1 t-sp sugar	Enough cooking oil

Thoroughly mince the meat, spring onion and ginger and mix them with 1½ t-sp soy sauce. Beat the eggs and add in the salt. Drop 2 tb-sp of cooking oil in the frying pan and when hot drop 1 tb-sp of the beaten egg in the centre of the pan in the same manner as frying griddle cakes. Immediately place 1 t-sp of meat mixture in the centre of the egg, fold over, press down edges, and remove from pan. Repeat the same process until all the ingredients are used up.

When all have been cooked replace in pan. Add ½ cup of water and remaining 1½ t-sp soy sauce and sugar. Cover tightly and cook slowly for 10 minutes and serve.

茶 蛋

Tea Eggs

20 eggs	1 tb-sp salt
½ cup soy sauce	1 star aniseed
3 oz. black tea	

Boil the eggs with all the ingredients in 2 bowls of water. After boiling for 10 minutes crack the shell of the eggs slightly without breaking the eggs. Boil for another 30 minutes and serve.

Egg

Chinese people serve this kind of tea eggs during the Chinese New Year. It is a good omen which will bring in or roll luck into one's home as the eggs can roll. It is also eaten during breakfast and afternoon tea. It is good for picnic parties.

Vegetables

蔬 菜

Chapter 8.　Vegetables

Chinese people are great vegetable eaters. There are a great variety of things that we eat, such as water melon rinds, radish and turnip tops, pea vines, etc. The vegetables in China are seasonal. Spring brings in horse beans, pea-pods and spring bamboo shoots. In summer and late autumn, different kinds of melons are sold in the markets. Green vegetables of different kinds are common in winter. Vegetables are not only used a great deal in China but the Chinese housewives and chefs are expert in producing vegetable dishes. Except for making soup, the Chinese do not cook vegetables with more water than is needed for a dish. Soft vegetables, such as lettuce, spinach and pea sprouts are best cooked in their own juice. For other hard vegetables use only as much water as is required to cover the vegetables in the frying pan. Water is always added after vegetables have been fried slightly with salt and covered with oil. Salt is used for most of the vegetable dishes and soy sauce is also used but comparatively little. In order to preserve the green colour and crispness, vegetables should not be covered with a lid during the process of cooking except when frying hard vegetables the lid may be used before water is added to the frying pan. For melons and hard beans, lids can be used until they are cooked.

In cooking vegetables, lard should always be used to make them taste better. Sometimes the vegetables are not even fried, they are carefully washed and rinsed with boiling water then mixed with salt, soy sauce and sesame oil. They are more crispy and their nutritive value is preserved. Always choose fresh vegetables in the market.

拌 糖 醋 炒 蘿 菠
Chinese Radish Salad

30 small radishes	1 tb-sp vinegar
1 t-sp salt	1½ tb-sp sugar
1 tb-sp soy sauce	2 t-sp sesame oil

Wash the radish and cut off both ends. Do not peel. Lay them face downward on a table and slightly crush them with the flat side of a knife or other heavy instrument. Do not break the radish into small pieces.

Vegetables

Mix in 1 t-sp salt and let it stand for 10 minutes. Then mix in the soy sauce, vinegar, sugar and sesame oil. Allow them to remain so for one quarter of an hour before serving.

If sesame oil is not obtainable salad oil or olive oil may be substituted.

The green tops of the radishes can be used as green vegetable. Wash them clean, and cut into ¼ inch sections. Mix with another t-sp salt and scrape hard. Then squeeze out the water. Fry them with 1½ tb-sp of lard or cooking oil in a pan. Stir on a hot fire for 1 minute and serve.

炒 菠 菜

Fried Spinach

1 lb. spinach
3 tb-sp lard
1 t-sp salt

Wash the spinach and drain all surplus moisture as much as possible because a great deal of water will come out of the spinach itself during the cooking. Do not cut the spinach if small. Cut the long ones into sections about 2 or 3 inches long, but do not remove stalks. Let the fat melt and spread over the whole frying pan, then fry the vegetable on a very strong heat and put in the salt immediately. Keep stirring for 3 minutes and it is done when the spinach becomes soft.

炒 冬 菰 豆 腐

Fried Mushrooms with Bean Curd

3 pieces bean curd
  (soft kind)
10 mushrooms
2 tb-sp soy sauce
½ t-sp sugar
2—3 spring onions
3 tb-sp lard

Wash the mushrooms and cut off the stems. Soak them in hot water. Heat the oil, cut the bean curd into pieces then fry them until they are brown on both sides. Pour in the mushroom, sugar and soy sauce. Add ½ cup of water in which the mushrooms were soaked. Cover the lid and simmer for 5 minutes.

Vegetables

炒 冬 瓜
Fried Winter Melon

1 lb. winter melon	1 t-sp sugar
4 tb-sp lard or cooking oil	1 t-sp sesame oil
1 tb-sp soy sauce	1 t-sp salt

Peel off the melon skin and cut the melon into 1 inch square. Heat the oil and fry the pieces for 2 or 3 minutes with salt. Pour the soy sauce and ½ cup of water into the skillet. Cook about 5 minutes on a slow fire. Mix with the sesame oil and serve.

芹 菜 炒 豆 芽
Fried Celery With Pea Sprout

½ lb. celery	1 t-sp sesame oil (optional)
½ lb. pea sprouts	1 t-sp salt
3 tb-sp lard	

Take off the leaves of the celery and throw away the tough parts. Cut into 1½ inches sections. Pick out the best pea sprout in the market and remove both ends. Drain off all the extra moisture from the celery and pea sprout after they have been washed.

Heat the lard in a frying pan until smoking hot, pour the celery in and stir for 1 minute. Immediately add in the pea sprouts and stir them together with salt for 2 minutes. Remove from pan and season with sesame oil if desired.

It is not advisable to fry the pea sprouts too long because much juice will ooze from the vegetables and discoloration will take place.

炒 芹 菜
Fried Celery

1 lb. celery	1 t-sp sesame oil (optional)
1 tb-sp soy sauce	3 tb-sp lard
½ t-sp salt	½ t-sp sugar

Remove the leaves of the celery and cut off the old stem. Cut into sections of 2 inches long and drain off the moisture after they have been washed. Heat the oil and fry the celery with salt. Keep stirring for 2 minutes, add the soy sauce and sugar. Mix them well then remove from pan. Serve with sesame oil if desired.

炒 黄 豆 芽
Fried Bean Sprouts

1 lb. sprouts	1 spring onion
4 tb-sp lard	3 slices ginger
½ t-sp salt	1 tb-sp soy sauce

Break off the roots from the bean sprouts and wash them under running water until they are rid of skins.

Heat the lard till hot and put in the bean sprouts with sliced ginger. Stir for 1 minute then add in salt. Cover the skillet and turn on a low fire. Let it cook for 5 minutes. Stir occasionally. Remove the cover and add the soy sauce and sectioned spring onions, then stir for 1 minute. During the process of cooking add a little water if necessary.

Bean sprouts are a by-product of soy beans. They can be grown at home with simple means provided the room temperature is accurately adjusted.

紅 烧 蘿 菠 絲
Braised Turnips

1 lb. turnips	1 spring onion
3 tb-sp lard	1 tb-sp soy sauce
½ t-sp salt	2—3 slices ginger

Peel the turnips and grate them. Heat the lard and fry for 1 minute then add the salt. Pour in 1 cup of water and simmer for 5 minutes with the lid on. Take off the cover and add the soy sauce and chopped spring onion and mix them thoroughly for 2 more minutes. Serve with pepper.

拌 蘿 菠 菜
Turnip Tops

1 lb. turnip tops	3 tb-sp lard
1 t-sp salt	

Vegetables

Wash the turnip tops thoroughly. Put in a boiler and pour in boiling water and cover the lid for 3 minutes. Take the turnip out and squeeze out the water. Cut them fine and fry in the lard on a high fire with salt for 2 minutes. While cooking stir constantly.

炒 碗 豆 苗
Fried Pea-Vines

1 lb. pea vines
3 tb-sp lard
1 t-sp salt
1 t-sp sugar

Pick up the tops of the pea-vines and throw away all the tough parts. Wash them clean and drain well. Heat the lard and fry the pea-vines with the salt on a brisk fire for 1 minute, add sugar and stir for another minute and serve.

奶 油 白 菜
Creamed Cabbage

1 lb. cabbage
3 tb-sp lard
1 t-sp cornflour
1 t-sp salt
½ cup evaporated milk
½ pint of stock
1 oz. minced ham

Wash the cabbage very clean. Cut into 2 inch squares. Put into boiling water for 3 minutes and drain. Heat the lard and fry the cabbage for 2 minutes with the salt, then pour in the stock or same amount of water. Dissolve the cornflour in the milk and pour into the pan also. Stir well and simmer for 5 minutes more. Sprinkle the minced ham and pepper on top. Serve piping hot.

炒 豇 豆
Fried Long Beans

1 lb. long beans
3 tb-sp lard
3 buds garlic
1 tb-sp soy sauce
½ t-sp salt

Snip off both ends of long beans, then break the long beans into sections about 1 inch long. Wash them clean.

Vegetables

Heat the lard and put in the crushed garlic buds and stir for ½ minute. Pour in the sectioned beans and stir for 1 minute with salt. Add ½ cup of water to the frying pan and cover the lid tightly. Cook for 5 minutes until the beans turn a fresh green colour. Then take off the cover and add in soy sauce and stir for another 5 minutes. When the water has bee almost evaporated the beans are cooked.

For this recipe if soy jam is used the flavour will be still better. Fry the soy jam with the crushed garlic before putting in the beans.

冬 筍 炒 扁 豆

Fried String Beans With Bamboo Shoots

½ lb. string beans
¼ lb. bamboo shoots
1 t-sp salt
½ t-sp sugar
3 tb-sp lard

Snip off both ends of the string beans and wash them clean.

Cut the bamboo shoots into slices. Heat the lard and fry the beans first. Stir for 2 minutes and add salt. Put in the bamboo shoots. Stir constantly for 1 minute more then add ½ cup of water. Cook over a low fire until the water is almost evaporated. Mix in the sugar and cook with the lid on for another minute or so. Mix in 1 t-sp of sesame oil before serving if desired.

蒸 茄 子

Steamed Eggplant

4 eggplants
½ t-sp salt
1 tb-sp soy sauce
1 t-sp sesame oil

Wash the eggplants and make a few slashes about ⅛ inch deep lengthwise, place them in a big bowl and steam them for 15 minutes with the lid cover on tightly. Use a pair of chopstick to tear them into long strips. Mix in the soy sauce, salt, sesame oil and serve. Chopped ginger and garlic may be added to suit individual taste.

蝦 米 拌 菠 菜

Dried Shrimps With Spinach

1 lb. spinach
2 oz. dried shrimps
1 t-sp salt
2 tb-sp sesame oil
2 tb-sp soy sauce

Vegetables

Wash the spinach but do not cut it. In a boilder put about 3 rice bowls of water and heat until boiling. Put in the spinach and heat again till the water starts to boil and drain. Pour about 1 bowl of cold boiled water on the spinach then drain the water away as much as possible. Chop the spinach.

Wash the dried shrimps and boil in 1 cup of water on a low fire for 10 minutes. Take out the shrimps and serve the water in which they were boiled. Chop the shrimps, mix with the chopped spinach, soy sauce, salt, sesame oil and the shrimps water. Serve cold.

炒 新 蠶 豆
Fried Fresh Horse Beans

2 lbs. horse beans
1 t-sp salt
4 tb-sp lard
½ lb. bamboo shoots
½ t-sp sugar

Shell and skin the beans and leave only the inner kernels. Heat half of the oil till hot and put in the beans. Add part of the salt and stir for 1 minute. Remove the outer skin of the bamboo shoots and cut into slices. Heat the remaining oil and fry the sliced bamboo shoots with the rest of the salt. Stir for 1 minute, add ¼ cup of water and mix in the beans and sugar. Fry them together for another 2 minutes and serve.

炒 碗 豆
Fried Fresh Peas

2 lbs. fresh peas in pods
6 tb-sp lard
1 t-sp salt

Shell the peas. Heat the lard till hot and fry the peas lightly in the hot oil and season with salt. Stir for 1 minute, add ¼ cup of water. Cover the pan with the lid and cook for another minute. When the water shows a tendency to dry up remove from pan and serve.

炒 生 菜
Fried Lettuce

1 lb. lettuce
5 tb-sp lard
1 t-sp salt
1 bud garlic

Vegetables

Wash the lettuce thoroughly. Heat the lard and put the crushed garlic in first and stir for ½ minute. Immediately pour in the lettuce and fry for one more minute with salt. When the leaves turn more green and soft it is ready to serve.

炒 南 瓜
Fried Pumpkin

1 lb. pumpkin	1 t-sp salt
5 tb-sp lard	

Peel the pumpkin and take out the seeds. Cut into 2 inch squares, and cut again crisscross on the back of the squares. Melt the lard till hot and fry the pumpkin in the oil with salt until tender and of a golden brown colour. Add ½ cup of water and simmer for another 10 minutes Serve with chopped spring onions.

蝦 米 炒 茄 子
Fried Eggplant With Dried Shrimps

½ lb. eggplant	½ t-sp salt
4 tb-sp lard	½ cup dried shrimps
1 tb-sp soy sauce	1 bud garlic

Cut the eggplant lengthwise into 2 sections, again into ½ inch thickness. Wash the dried shrimps and soak them in ½ cup of hot water. Peel off the outer skin of the garlic and crush it. Heat the cooking oil and fry the eggplant with salt and crushed garlic for 2 minutes. Add dried shrimps with ½ cup of water in which they were soaked. Cook under a low fire about 10 minutes then add the soy sauce and simmer for another 5 minutes and serve.

炒 素 冬 菰
Fried Mushrooms

30 big mushrooms	6 tb-sp lard
1 t-sp salt	1 tb-sp cornflour

Wash the mushrooms and cut off the stems. Soak them in 1 cup of hot water 1 hour before the cooking. Heat the lard till hot, pour in the mushrooms and fry them with salt for 2 minutes. Then add the cup of

Vegetables

water in which the mushrooms were soaked. Cook continuously for 10 minutes with the lid on. Mix the cornflour with a little water and pour into the pan. Stir well and serve.

冬 筍 炒 冬 菰

Fried Mushrooms With Bamboo Shoots

15 mushrooms	½ t-sp salt
1 lb. bamboo shoots	1 tb-sp soy sauce
6 tb-sp lard	1 tb-sp cornflour

Use the same method as the preceding recipe to clean and soak the mushrooms. Heat ½ the lard and fry the mushrooms for 2 minutes then remove from pan. Remove the outer skin of the bamboo shoots and throw away the old parts. Cut the rest into thin slices. Heat the remaining lard and fry the sliced bamboo shoots for 4 minutes with salt then mix in the mushrooms. Add soy sauce and stir for a while. Pour in the mushroom water and cook for 10 minutes with the lid on. Mix the cornflour with a little water and put into the frying pan. Heat until boiling. Arrange the mushrooms on top of the bamboo shoots while serving.

奶 油 冬 菰

Creamed Bamboo Shoots

3 lbs. bamboo shoots	½ cup evaporated milk
6 tb-sp lard	½ pint of stock
1 t-sp cornflour	1 oz. minced ham
1 t-sp salt	

Remove the skins of the bamboo shoots. Cut off the tough parts, then slice them. Heat the lard and fry the sliced bamboo shoots for 3 minutes with salt, then pour in the stock or same amount of water. Cook for 5 minutes. Dissolve the cornflour in the milk and pour into the pan also. Stir well and simmer for 5 minutes more. Mix in the cooked minced ham and serve piping hot.

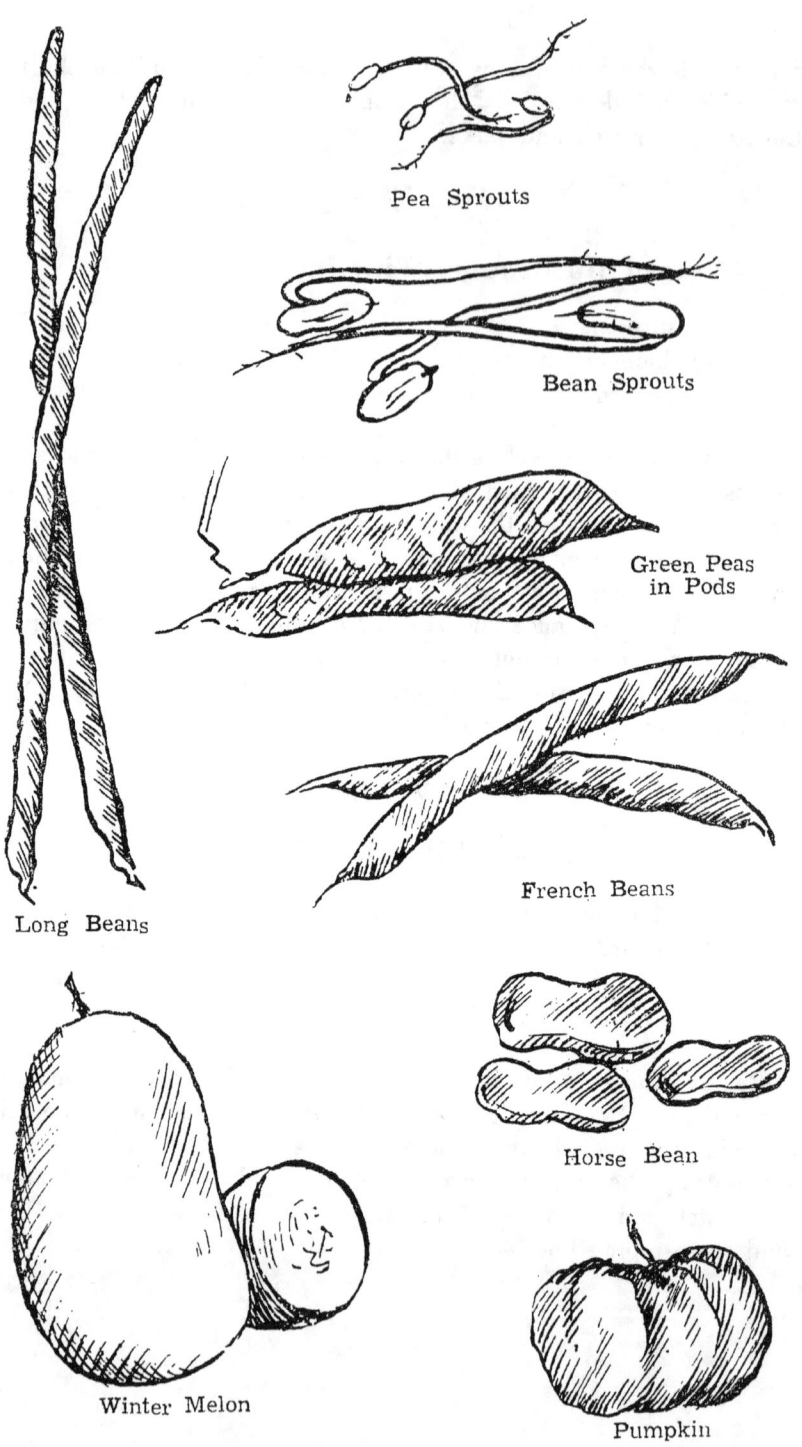

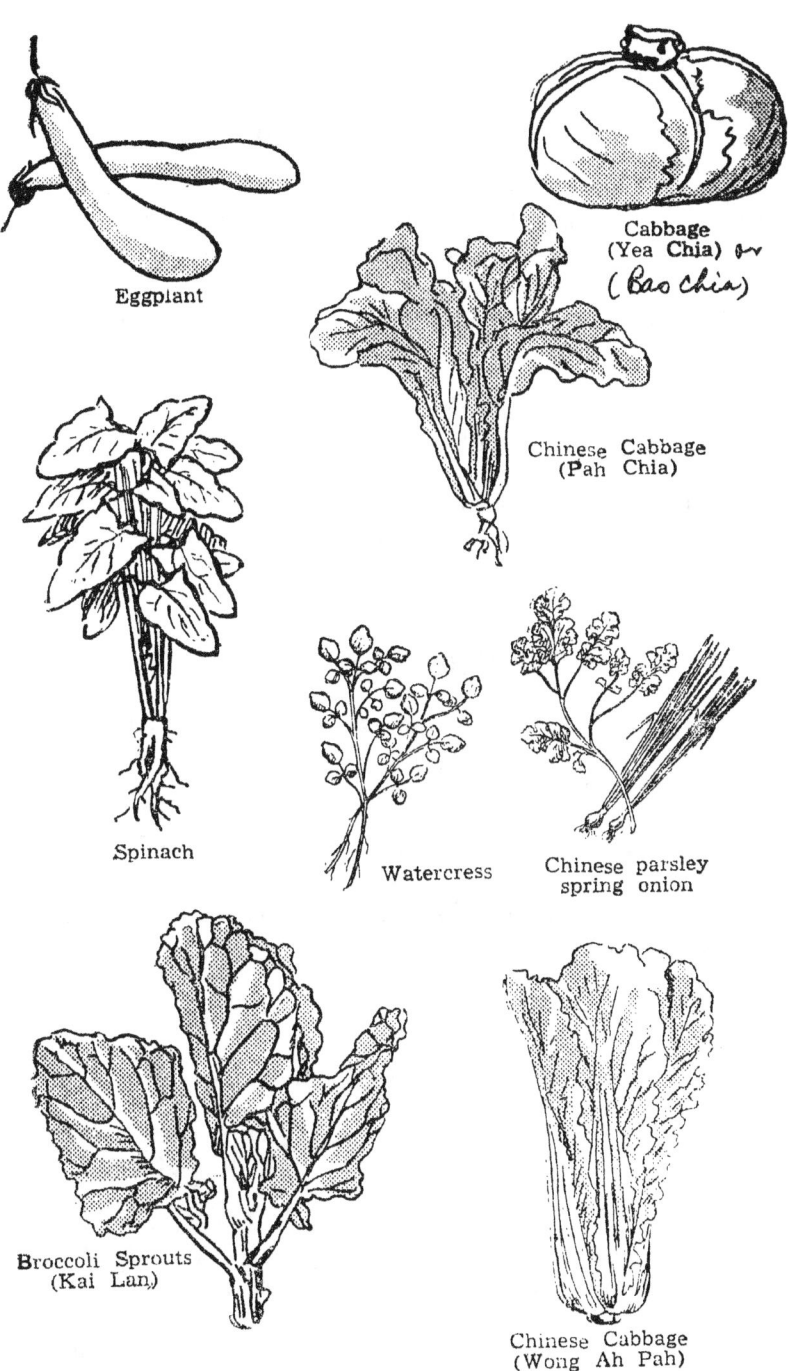

Soup

湯

Chapter 9. Soup

Soup is taken during or after meals according to Chinese custom but never before meals. The soup is placed in the centre of the table along with the other dishes round it, the diners taking some whenever they wish. It is the usual practice that soup is served several times in Chinese banquets but only once served in family meals though the soup bowl is sometimes refilled several times at one meal.

A heavy soup made with meat ingredients requires some boiling whereas a light soup made with vegetables requires a shorter time.

Chafing dish may be classified as either soup or as a main dish. There is no soup served, however, when the chafing dish is on the table.

雞 湯

Chicken Soup

1 hen (3 or 4 lbs.)　　　　1 tb-sp sherry (optional)
1½ tb-sp salt　　　　　　2—3 slices ginger
1 spring onion

Singe, draw and wash the chicken thoroughly and put in a heavy pot with 2½ pints of cold water. Heat over a big fire until it boils. Then add the spring onion, salt and ginger and turn to a low fire to simmer with the lid on for 3 hours.

白 木 耳 雞 湯

White Fungis And Chicken Soup

1 hen　　　　　　　　　1 oz. white fungis
1 tb-sp salt　　　　　　1 tb-sp sherry (optional)

Singe and draw the chicken from the tail. Wash it clean. Break the legs and place in a boiler with 2½ pints of water and boil on a low fire for 2½ hours after the water has started to boil.

Soak the white fungis in water for 3 hours. Pick out the black stuff from the white fungis and wash away all the sand. Put them in a

Soup

bowl with enough water to cover them up and steam on a low fire for 2 hours. Pour into the chicken soup and boil them together on a low fire for 10 minutes. Add salt and place the whole chicken in a big soup bowl with the white fungis around it and serve.

冬 菰 鴨 湯

Duck Soup

1 duck	20 mushrooms (big)
1 tb-sp salt	¼ lb. ham
½ lb. bamboo shoots	2—3 slices ginger

Singe and draw the duck. Remove the oil sacs. Put it into a heavy pot with 2½ pints of water and boil over a big fire. Skim the scum after boiling and turn on a low fire and cook for 2 hours. Add the whole piece of ham, sliced bamboo shoots, mushrooms, ginger and salt and continue to boil for another ½ hour or more. Test with a fork and if the bird is still tough cook for another ½ hour. Take out the whole piece of ham and cut it into thin slices when it is cold and firm. Put it on the top of the duck with the sliced bamboo shoots. Serve the soup hot.

燉 牛 肉 湯

Steamed Beef Soup

1 lb. soup beef (shin)	2—3 slices ginger
½ tb-sp salt	1 spring onion

Cut the beef into big pieces and put in a double boiler with the spring onion, ginger and salt. Heat 1 quart of water until it boil and pour into the double boiler. Continue to heat on a low fire for 5 hours. Serve with pepper.

蘿 菠 牛 肉 湯

Beef And Turnip Soup

1 lb. muscle meat	1 tb-sp salt
½ lb. turnip	1 spring onion
2—3 slices ginger	

Peel the turnips and cut them into squares. Cut the meat into fairly large pieces or about the sizes of the turnips. Simmer in 2½ pints of water on a low fire for 2 hours after water has started to boil then add in the turnips and ginger. Keep on a low fire for 1½ hours more. Add salt and chopped spring onions and serve.

排 骨 蕃 薯 湯

Potato And Pork-Bone Soup

1 lb. pork-bone	½ lb. tomatoes
½ lb. potatoes	1 tb-sp salt

Wash the bones and place them in a heavy pot with 2½ pints of water and boil on high fire until boiling. After it starts to boil, skim the scum and then turn to a low fire and boil for 1 hour continuously. Peel the potatoes and cut both potatoes and tomatoes into large pieces and place with the bones in the pot for boiling. Simmer for another ½ hour and serve with salt.

猪 肺 湯

Pig's Lung Soup

1 lung	1 tb-sp sherry (optional)
½ cup barley	3—4 slices ginger
20 mushrooms	2 t-sp salt

Put the lung under running cold water, fill up lungs and let the water run through the vessels until it is free of blood. Cut it into pieces. Put them into a frying pan and heat on a low fire until the water is dried. Stir constantly while heating. Put them back in a heavy boiler with 2½ pints of water, barley, sherry, ginger and mushrooms and simmer on a low heat for 2 hours. Serve with pepper and salt.

猪 腦 湯

Pig's Brain Soup

4 pairs pig brains	1½ pints chicken soup or pork bone soup
10 sliced mushrooms	
1 cup grated turnip	1½ t-sp salt
1 tb-sp sherry (optional)	1 spring onion

Wash the brains thoroughly in salt and warm water. Boil the grated turnips in the chicken soup for ½ hour then add the sliced mushrooms

Soup

and brains. Put in the rest of the ingredients when it is boiling again for 10 minutes before serving.

燉 豬 肝 湯
Steamed Liver Soup

½ lb. liver
¼ lb. pork
¼ lb. ham

½ tb-sp salt
2—3 slices ginger
2—3 spring onions

The pork selected should be lean. Cut the liver, pork and ham into slices. Put them in a double boiler with salt, ginger and spring onion. Heat 1½ pints of water until it boils and pour into a double boiler and steam on a low fire for 4 hours. Season with pepper, salt and serve.

豬 腳 湯
Pig's Trotter Soup

2 trotters
½ lb. turnips

1 tb-sp salt
2—3 spring onions

Clean the trotters and pull off all the hair. Wash and cut them into large pieces. Simmer in 2½ pints of water for 1 hour. Cut the turnips in large squares and boil them together for 2 hours on a low fire. Add the salt during the process of simmering. Serve with chopped spring onion and pepper according to the taste of different individuals.

豬 骨 湯 — 雞 骨 湯
Pork-Bone Or Chicken-Bone Soup

1 lb. pork bone or chicken bone

2½ pints water
1 tb-sp salt

Put the bones in a heavy pot with the water. Heat over a high fire until boiling. Remove to a lower fire and continue to simmer for 2 to 3 hours. Skim the scum.

This is a soup which can be used as basic soup in which shark's fins, bird nest, vegetables, etc., can be added. Pork bones can be served at table but not the chicken bones.

Soup

冬 菰 蠶 豆 湯
Mushrooms With Horse Bean Soup

1 lb. horse beans	½ tb-sp salt
10 big mushrooms	½ tb-sp sesame oil or lard
2 tb-sp soy sauce	

Peel and skin the beans then put them in a bowl and steam for 10 minutes with ½ t-sp salt.

Cut off the stems of the mushrooms and wash. Soak in hot water. Put them in a big soup bowl with soy sauce and water and steam for ½ hour after the water has started to boil. Mix in the sesame oil or lard, salt, and the horse beans before serving.

冬 菰 雞 絲 湯
Chicken Shreds And Mushroom Soup

2 oz. chicken breast	2 oz. ham
10 mushrooms	1 spring onion
2 oz. cabbage	1 tb-sp soy sauce
½ t-sp salt	

Pick out the hearts of the cabbage and wash them clean. Cut the mushrooms and shred the ham and chicken meat. The mushrooms must be previously washed and soaked in hot water before cutting. Heat 1 pint of water and boil the vegetable, mushroom and ham for 3 minutes. Add the meat of the chicken and keep boiling until the meat turns white. Pour in the soy sauce, salt and chopped spring onion before serving.

菠 菜 豬 肝 湯
Spinach And Pig's Liver Soup

¼ lb. liver	1 tb-sp soy sauce
½ lb. spinach	1 t-sp salt
1 t-sp lard	1 pint of stock

Wash the spinach and cut into 2 or 3 sections if they are big ones. Again cut the liver into thin slices and soak them in the soy sauce. Boil the water or heat the stock till it boils, add the lard and salt to it. As

Soup

soon as it boils put in the spinach, seasoned liver and sliced ginger. Leave it on the fire for 2 more minutes and serve.

猪 腰 湯

Kidney Soup

2 kidneys	2 oz. mushrooms
1 tb-sp soy sauce	1 tb-sp lard
1 t-sp salt	1 tb-sp cornflour

Cut the kidney into halves and remove the gristle of the kidney. Again cut into pieces then cut crisscross on the surface. Mix well with the cornflour and soy sauce.

Wash the mushrooms and slice them. Fry the sliced mushroom for 2 minutes, then add 1 pint of hot stock or boiling water. When it is boiling put in the sliced kidney and salt. Serve after boiling.

魚 湯

Fish Soup

1 bass	1 tb-sp lard
3—4 spring onions	2—3 slices ginger
1 bowl chicken soup	2 t-sp salt

Scale the bass and take off the gills. From the head of the bass draw everything out but save the lung. Wash the fish and the lung thoroughly. Heat the chicken soup to boiling point and put in the bass, ginger and spring onion and cook under a low fire till boiling. After 10 minutes, add the lung of the bass, lard and salt. Cook for another 10 minutes and serve with pepper.

魚 頭 蘿 菠 湯

Fish Head And Turnip Soup

1 large fish head	3—4 slices ginger
½ lb. turnips	1 tb-sp lard
1 t-sp sherry (optional)	½ tb-sp salt
3—4 spring onions	

Peel and grate the turnips. Wash the fish and remove the gills. Heat the lard and fry the head on both sides for 5 minutes, add salt, ginger,

Soup

spring onion and sherry. Put it in a heavy boiler with 2 pints of cold water and boil over a high fire till boiling. Remove to a low fire and boil for ½ hour then add the grated turnip. Boil continuously for another 1 hour until the grated turnips are tender and the soup obtains a creamy colour. Season pepper.

肉 丸 粉 絲 湯
Meat Ball And Chinese Vermicelli Soup

½ lb. pork	1 t-sp cornflour
1 tb-sp soy sauce	2 t-sp salt
1 oz Chinese vermicelli	1 spring onion

The pork selected should be fairly fat. Mince the pork and mix thoroughly with cornflour, ½ t-sp salt and 2 tb-sp water. This mixture should be made into small meat balls about the size of pigeon eggs.

Wash the vermicelli in water and put into 1½ pints of water or stock to boil for 5 minutes. Drop in the meat balls and keep it boiling for 2 or 3 minutes more. Pour in the chopped spring onion, salt and the soy sauce, season with pepper and serve,

菠 菜 湯
Spinach Soup

½ lb. spinach	½ tb-sp salt
1 bamboo shoot	1 tb-sp sesame oil
4 mushrooms	

Select the best young spinach in the market and throw away the yellow leaves. Wash the spinach and cut into sections if they are too big or if they are more than 2 inches long. Cut the bamboo shoots into thin slices and wash the mushrooms before cooking. Save the water in which the mushrooms were soaked. Boil 1 pint of water with the mushroom water and pour in the mushrooms and bamboo slices. Boil for 10 minutes. Add spinach and salt and boil continously 1 minute longer. Mix in the sesame oil or lard and serve.

冬 菰 雞 蛋 湯
Egg And Mushroom Soup

2 eggs	½ t-sp salt
5 mushrooms	½ tb-sp lard
1 tb-sp soy sauce	

Wash the mushrooms and soak them in a cup of hot water. Beat the eggs. Bring 1 pint of stock or water to the boil and add the mushrooms

Soup

with the water in which they are soaked. Keep on boiling for 5 minutes, add the salt, lard, soy sauce and the beaten eggs.

Two or three fresh or tinned tomatoes can be added if desired but boil the sliced tomatoes with the mushrooms for 5 minutes before pouring the eggs into the soup.

青 燉 冬 菰 湯

Steamed Mushroom Soup

20 big mushrooms   1½ t-sp salt

Cut off the stems of the mushrooms and wash clean. Soak in hot water before cooking. Warm up about 1 pint of plain chicken soup and add the soaked mushrooms with the water in which they are soaked. Steam them on a low fire for about 1 hour. Add salt and serve.

冬 菰 豆 腐 湯

Mushroom And Bean Curd Soup

8 mushrooms   ½ lb. bamboo shoots
1 piece bean curd (soft kind)   ½ tb-sp salt
½ lb. bamboo shoots   ½ tb-sp lard

Wash and cut off the stems of the mushrooms. Soak them in 1½ pints of water before cooking. Boil the mushroom for 10 minutes in the water. Cut the bean curd into pieces and take off the skin of the bamboo shoots then cut into thin slices. Add the bean curd and bamboo shoots to the mushroom soup and boil for 5 minutes more. Add salt, lard and serve.

青 菜 豆 腐 湯

Cabbage And Bean Curd Soup

4 oz. cabbage heart   1 tb-sp lard
2 pieces bean curd (soft kind)   1 tb-sp salt

Select the best part of the cabbage and wash clean. Heat the lard and fry the cabbage with ½ tb-sp of salt for 3 minutes. Cut the bean curd in small pieces and add to the cabbage and stir slightly for 1 minute. Add 1½ pints of water and the remaining salt and boil for 5 minutes.

Soup

濃 湯
Thick Soup

6 eggs	¾ cup lard
½ cup shrimps	½ cup sherry (optional)
½ cup ham	1 t-sp cornflour
½ lb. bamboo shoots	½ tb-sp salt

Beat the eggs and shell the shrimps and wash them clean. Dice the ham and bamboo shoots then soak in a cup of water for 3 minutes. With a pair of chopsticks or fork mix thoroughly together with the eggs, 1 cup chicken stock, cornflour, salt and sherry. Put the lard in a frying pan and place over a medium fire Add the above ingredients, increase the heat, and stir the mixture constanly. As soon as the mixture turns into a creamy consistency quickly add the shrimps, diced ham and bamboo shoots.

This dish requires very careful attention as the secret of its making lies in the mixture not being permitted to become lumpy. Only quick action will guarantee good results. This dish may be served either with rice or noodles.

西 洋 菜 湯
Watercress Soup

½ lb. watercress	1 tb-sp salt
½ lb. lean pork	2 slices ginger

Cut the pork into squares. Put into a heavy pot and boil with 2 pints of water and 2 slices of ginger for ½ hour.

Pick out the green leaves of the watercress and throw away the stems. Put the leaves into the pot and boil together with the pork for another 10 minutes. Add salt and serve.

The Chinese Chafing Dishes

中 國 火 鍋

The Chinese Chafing Dish

The term *Ke-tze* in Chinese means chafing dish. This Chinese utensil is dissimilar in construction to those of other countries. It possesses on an entirely different heating unit. A flue or chimney, penetrates the centre of the native chafing dish and charcoal burned at the base above the grate supplies the necessary heat. There is another type which is similar to this with the exception that, the chafing dish is supported by a 5 inches wide and 3 inches long high hollow circular collar of brass, which in turn rests on a brass plate. Different fancy designs have been cut into the collar, a cup which contains alcohol is placed in the collar and under the chafing dish. The lighting of the alcohol will not only cause the fire to strike the bottom of the chafing dish but also to escape through the lattice work in the collar to heat all sides of the basin. The brass plate and the collar of the chafing dish are all always placed on the table, and then the basin, with the water or the soup, is brought in and placed on top of the collar. The use of the modern electric hot plate underneath a large pot or basin would overcome the inconveniences of obtaining the Chinese Chafing dish.

There are two ways of preparing the chafing dish. The first way is to cook everything in another boiler, and then transfer to the chafing dish; the burning charcoal is packed into the base about the grate and fanned glowing red; and then the chafing dish with all the ingredients is brought to the table. The guests then help themselves to bowlfuls of the ingredients and the soup. A similar way can be done with the alcohol type. The second way is particularly attractive and unique due to the fact that the diners prepare their own food, selecting from the variety of ingredients which surround the chafing dish. Individual bowls are served at the moment the food is cooked to form the basis of the meal.

什 錦 火 鍋

Ten Variety Chafing Dish

The First Method. The following Ten Variety Chafing Dish is always pre-cooked.

    1. Meat balls. 1 lb. ground pork, or sausage meat — mix thoroughly with chopped spring onions, the top of the spring

The Chinese Chafing Dishes

onions should be used as well as the white portions. Add ¼ t-sp of chopped ginger, 2 tb-sp cornflour and 1 tb-sp soy sauce. Mix them thoroughly and make into little balls about 1 inch in thickness. Fry to a golden brown in 4 tb-sp lard, piping hot.

2. Cabbage. Cut 1 lb. cabbage into shreds.
3. Fish balls. 1 to 2 dozens—see *page 43*.
4. Braised chicken.

   1 chicken   2 t-sp salt
   6 tb-sp soy sauce

   Put everything in a pot. Heat over big fire 6 cups of water till boiling then pour into the pot. Simmer for 1 hour on a low fire. If the chicken is not tender, boil it for another hour or more. Then take out the chicken and chop into enough pieces to go round. Keep the gravy for another use in this recipe.

5. Chinese vermicelli or pea-starch noodles. Soak in warm water and let it stand in water before using.
6. Egg wrapping (or Dumplings). 10—15 in number see *page 90*.
7. Winter bamboo shoots. Cut up into slices—canned or fresh.
8. Ham. Chinese ham or any other ham obtainable in the market.
9. Abalone. 1 tin—cut them into slices.
10. Bean curd. 4 pieces (soft kind).

These ten varieties are all placed in the pot in many layers. The order of the layers from the bottom up is as follow: cabbage shreds, bean curd, braised chicken, meat balls, peastarch noodles, egg wrappings, abalone, ham, bamboo shoots and fish balls. Spread the ham slices and the bamboo slices by over-lapping each slice a little. Then drop the fish ball around on the top of the chafing dish.

Finally pour in the gravy of the braised chicken. Cook the whole pot in the kitchen over a low fire for about ½ hour. Then bring the dish to the dining table and heat continuously. Add a little water to the chafing dish from time to time to prevent it from burning or from getting too dry. Put the fire out when the contents in the chafing dish are about to finish.

The Chinese Chafing Dishes

The Second Method. Chafing Dish of this kind in not pre-cooked.

1. Small chicken. Slice and arranged on plate in an attractive manner.
2. Chicken soup this can be made from chicken carcass after the meat has been carved away.
3. ¼ lb Chinese vermicelli or Pea-starch Noodles—soak in warm water for ½ hour before placing on a plate.
4. 1 lb. fish. Thinly sliced and arranged on a plate.
5. 1 lb. spinach. Wash and place on a big plate. There are other small vegetables which could be similarly employed, but, of course, it is a matter of individual fancy.
6. 1 lb. liver. Sliced and arranged on a plate.
7. 1 pair kidneys.—sliced and washed thoroughly; all the white gristle should be cut away.
8. 10 eggs.
9. Spring onion. ½ lb.—sectioned and put on a plate.
10. 1 lb. pork tenderloin.—sliced and arranged nicely on the plate.

Assuming that sliced chicken, sectioned spring onions, Chinese vermicelli, sliced liver, kidney, fish, pork and soy sauce have been previously prepared and made ready, these dishes are placed around the chafing dish which is in the centre of the table. Chicken stock is brought to a boil in the chafing dish. The vermicelli is then added. When the liquid again boils each diner select portions of the chafing dish directly opposite to him. The length of time required to cook each item is very short and as the ingredients food is consumed, more is gradually added, thus maintaining a constant supply. More soup can also be added but care should be taken not to add too much toward the end of the meal as the concentrated soup which remains is very delicious when used to moisten the rice which is served last.

It is the customary to break a raw egg in each bowl and pour the soup, the ingredients and soy sauce on it. This however is a matter of individual taste and the diners should be permitted to suit their own fancy.

Attractive garnishing of the raw ingredients greatly adds to the appearance of the chafing dish.

The Chinese Chafing Dishes

菊 花 火 鍋

Chrysanthemum Fish Chafing Dish

The Chrysanthemum Fish Chafing Dish is also not a pre-cooked method. The following are the main ingredients:

1. Big head of white chrysanthemum flower. Take off the petals and wash them clean.
2. 3 lbs. carp, perch, bass, turbot. or flounder. Either of these fish fillet will be suitable. Scale the fish and slice into thin pieces. Arrange them on a big plate.
3. 1 lb. spinach—wash them clean and put them on a big plate.
4. 2 lbs. bamboo shoots.—sliced them very thinly and arrange them on a big plate.
5. ½ lb. vermicelli—soak them in hot water before placing them on a plate.
6. ¾ cup sherry (optional).
7. ½ cup lard.
8. Eggs. The number is according to the number of persons dining.
9. 2 t-sp salt.

Divide each of the ingredients into two parts and place each part in a small plate. Arrange the fish slices symmetrically.

When it is the time to eat mix the fish slices with ½ cup of soy sauce and some chopped spring onions. Bring the chafing dish which contains chicken soup, salt and lard, to the centre of the table. The diners use chopsticks and help to put the vegetables, vermicelli, etc., into the pot. When the soup boils again, each diner helps himself from the big pot into his own bowl. Now the host or hostess puts in the chrysanthemum. Then salt is added, diners break eggs in their own bowls and pour the hot soup over it, or beat an egg in the bowl and pour the hot soup on it or even poach the egg in the big pot itself. Dip the food from the pot in soy sauce according to the taste of each individual.

Sandy-Pots

沙 鍋
Sandy-Pot

In China, a special chafing dish make by mixing sand and cast iron and cast very thin is used to cook beans curd or fish head and it is called Sandy-Pot which is usually served on table. Any kind of heavy pot can serve for the same purpose. The pot is placed on the table because there is plenty of gravy in it so it is very hard to transfer to some other utensil.

沙 鍋 魚 頭
Sandy-Pot Fish Head

1 big fish head	1 t-sp salt
½ lb. pork	2 tb-sp soy sauce
½ lb. bamboo shoots	2—3 slices ginger
½ lb. mushrooms	2 spring onions

Wash and soak the mushrooms in hot water. Slice the bamboo shoots and ham. Heat the lard in a skillet and fry the head for 5 minutes on both sides. Put in a Sandy-pot or a heavy pot with 2 cups of water and cook for 20 minutes. Add salt, ginger, spring onion, mushroom, bamboo shoots, meat slices, ham and cook for another 20 minutes. Place the Sandy-pot in which the fish head is cooked on the table.

沙 鍋 豆 腐
Sandy-Pot Bean Curd

6 pieces bean curd (soft kind)	2 tb-sp lard
	¼ lb. mushrooms
½ lb. pork	2—3 spring onions
2 tb-sp soy sauce	1 t-sp salt

Cut the pork into thin slices and remove the stems of the mushrooms. Wash them and soak them in 2 cups of water before using.

Cut the bean curd into pieces of about 2 inches by 1½ inches. Put in a big sandy-pot with 2 bowls of water. Use a big fire and boil for ½ hour. Add soy sauce, meat slices, mushroom and salt and cook till boiling, then simmer for another 20 minutes and serve in the sandy-pot.

飯

Chapter 10. Rice

Rice is the staple food of Southern China. In the Northern provinces, wheat and other grain are eaten more than rice.

There are two kinds of rice, glutinous rice and the ordinary rice. Both can be obtained in powder form. The former when eaten in excess, is hard to digest and is not suitable for young children or invalids. The ordinary rice is generally eaten two or three times a day by some people. There are two kinds, long-grained and oval-grained. The long-grained is easier to cook. Oval-grained is harder to cook and is eaten by the people living along the coastal provinces.

There are also two forms of rice as finished food, dry rice and soft rice. Dry rice is the usual main food of a meal and is prepared by boiling or steaming. The soft rice, called congee or rice gruel by English-speaking people in the East, is made by boiling very little rice in a large quantity of water. It is used as breakfast in the morning by most Chinese people, but some take it at night as dessert cooked in various forms. It is good for old people and invalids or when one does not feel hungry or strong enough to eat dry boiled rice.

There are perhaps hundreds of recipes for boiled rice. Although the various processes differ somewhat, nevertheless the ultimate purpose, to produce rice which is thoroughly cooked, attractive in appearance, and having each grain separate, is the same. There is a great variation in personal preference as to the hardness or softness of rice. In any event, properly cooked rice should be dry and uniform in texture. Even the softest rice should have all moisture completely absorbed into each grain and not left between the grains.

Two things are most essential, regardless of the process employed. First, the rice itself must be of a fine quality. Rice grown in Korea and Formosa is considered the best obtainable. Secondly, the choice of utensils for the cooking of rice is very important. One made of a combination of brass and copper is regarded by the Chinese as ideal for the purpose.

Rice is called "fan" after it has been cooked, boiled or steamed. Oval-grained rice is better when steamed, but either method can be used for either kind of grain.

Rice

煑 飯
Boiled Rice

1 cup rice   2 cups water

For cooking dry rice, the proportion is 1 cup of rice to 2 cups of water or the water should be 1 inch higher than the rice. Half a cup to 1 cup of water may be added if soft rice is desired, however, less than 2 cups of water will make the rice under-cooked and more than 3 cups of water will cause the rice to be burnt. First of all, wash the rice and drain off the water. Add 2—3 cups of water and boil over a big fire. It will make no difference whether the rice is added after boiling or before boiling. Turn to a very low fire after boiling or as soon as all the visible water has been boiled away. Cover and cook about 20 minutes or until steam is visible round the edge of the lid. When it is well cooked the rice is soft and dry and give no wet, shining appearance.

蒸 飯
Steamed Rice

There are several methods to cook dry steamed rice.

a. Steamed rice in Chungking, Kweichow and Changsha style.

1 cup rice   2—3 cups water

Wash the rice and drain off the water, add 3 cups of water and boil for 3 minutes after boiling. Drain off the rice soup. Put the rice in a rice steamer and steam for 30 minutes to 1 hour.

> *b.* Steamed rice in Cantonese style. The rice is steamed in a bowl instead of a rice steamer. Use the same amount of rice and water, as in the dry-steamed rice in the preceding recipe. Boil for five minutes; then drain off the rice soup and put the rice which is half-cooked in individual bowls only ¾ full so that there is room for the rice to expand. Steam over medium fire for 1 to 1½ hours. Be sure to have enough steaming water, but don't let it get directly into the bowls To prevent this, add water gradually and constantly allowing only enough to steam.

The great disadvantage of this method lies in having to pour the rice soup away. The rice soup is very nutritious and very good served as a drink when mixed with sugar. It is not advisable to wash the rice after

Rice

the water is boiling and it is not advisable also to pour the valuable rice soup away, though the steamed rice usually has a loose, pleasant texture. However, the advantage of this method is that there is no danger of rice being burnt in the final stage of cooking.

火 腿 菜 飯

Cabbage and Ham Rice

½ lb. rice
2 tb-sp lard
4 ozs. ham

½ lb. cabbage
2 t-sp salt

Wash the cabbage and chop both the ham and cabbage. After the rice is washed put the usual amount of water and cook. While it is boiling mix in salt, lard, ham and chopped cabbage, and mix thoroughly. Cover tight and cook until all the water is gone. Turn on a low fire and heat for 15 minutes. Serve hot.

During the process of heating special attention must be paid because it is the time when rice can very easily be burnt.

什 錦 炒 飯

Assorted Fried Rice

½ lb. rice
6 eggs
¼ lb. ham
4—6 mushrooms
2 t-sp salt

½ lb. sausage
½ lb. shrimps
½ cup peas
8 tb-sp lard

Cook the rice first. Soak the mushrooms in hot water for 10 minutes. Cut off the stems and then dice them. Beat the eggs and add 1 t-sp salt and stir well. Heat 2 tb-sp lard and fry the well beaten eggs for 1 minute. Remove from fire. Heat again another 2 tb-sp of lard and add sliced mushrooms, ham dices and peas. After 5 minutes remove from fire. Finally fry the well cooked rice with 4 tb-sp of heated lard and mix with the cooked eggs, sausage, shrimps, peas, mushrooms, ham and 1 t-sp salt. Stir constantly for 2 minutes and serve.

Rice

雞 蛋 泡 飯
Egg And Rice

3 eggs	2 slices bamboo shoots
2 tb-sp lard	2 slices ham
2 bowls cooked rice	½ t-sp salt
1 bowl chicken soup	

Put the lard in a pan and bring it to boiling point. Add eggs which have been well beaten with salt, and with a pair of chopsticks stir for a moment until the contents begin to thicken slightly. Then quickly add the cooked rice and stir well. Put in one slice of minced ham and chicken soup and cook until the dish is hot. Remove from fire, place in a bowl, garnish with the remaining slice of minced ham and bamboo shoots which have previously been cooked with a little salt. Season with pepper and serve.

火 腿 雞 蛋 炒 飯
Fried Ham And Egg Rice

2 eggs	4 tb-sp lard
1 oz. ham	1 t-sp salt
2 bowls cooked rice	2 spring onions

Beat the eggs and add ½ t-sp salt. Heat the lard till hot and fry the eggs. Stir them fast and then add in the cooked rice and stir constantly until well mixed. Pour in the chopped ham, spring onion and ½ t-sp salt. While chopping the ham save a few slices. Arrange the sliced ham on the top of the fried rice and serve.

白 粥
White Congee

½ cup rice	4 cups waters

Wash the rice and put in a boiler with 4 cups of water and bring to the boil. Turn to a low fire and simmer until the whole thing becomes a nearly uniform mess like oatmeal. The best rice for congee is a kind of semi-glutinous fragrant rice grown in lower Kiangsu Province or the new rice of each season because such rice is more sticky than old rice.

In the morning Chinese usually eat white congee with a few accompanying dishes for breakfast. When babies start to eat rice they start with soft rice.

Rice

雞 粥

Chicken Congee

1 young chicken	4 tb-sp soy sauce
¼ cup rice	2—3 spring onions
¼ cup glutinous rice	4 tb-sp sherry (optional)
1 tb-sp salt	2—3 slices ginger

Dress and clean the chicken and cut it into two. Boil it in a heavy boiler on a low fire with 2½ pints of boiling water, spring onions and ginger. When the chicken is half-cooked, add the sherry and salt. Simmer continously for ½ hour more. Take the chicken out from the boiler and cut each portion into pieces. Wash both the glutinous rice and rice and boil them in the chicken soup. When the rice forms a uniform mess like oatmeal, divide the chicken pieces among the bowls and put 1 tb-sp soy sauce in each of them. Pour the congee into the bowls and season with pepper and chopped ginger according to individual taste.

羅 漢 粥

Buddha Congee

1 cup rice	2 ozs. scallop
2 ozs. dried shrimps	2 tb-sp salt
2 ozs. cooked ham	2 tb-sp lard
2 ozs. cooked chicken meat	4 tb-sp sherry (optional)

Wash the dried shrimps and remove the heads and shells, Soak the scallops in the sherry or water and tear them into shreds Mince both the cooked ham and chicken and mix them together. Wash the rice and boil in 6 cups of water or chicken soup on a low fire. Keep it boiling for ½ hour then add in the mixture and lard. Boil for another ½ hour. Season with salt and serve.

It is called Buddha congee because of the varieties of condiments in cooking the congee.

蝦 粥

Shrimp Congee

4 ozs. shrimps	2 ozs. ham
¼ cup glutinous rice	1 tb-sp salt
¼ cup rice	

Rice

Wash both the rice and glutinous rice and boil them in 6 cups of water on a low fire. Remove the head and shells of the shrimps. Shred the ham and place in the boiler with the shrimps. Continue to boil until the rice becomes a uniform mess like oatmeal. Add 1 tb-sp of salt and season with pepper.

Noodles

麵

Chapter 11. Noodles

Noodles are eaten in different ways such as soup noodles, fried noodles, mixed noodles, etc. For the benefit of the inexperienced it should be stated that the word "noodles" implies, many different preparations of noodles. It may be of interest to list a few of more important or popular varieties of the fried noodles.

1. Fried Ham Noodles.
2. Fried Shrimp Noodles.
3. Fried Chicken Noodles.
4. Fried Meat Shred Noodles.
5. Fried Mushroom Noodles.

There are only a few varieties of soup noodles. Soup noodles served in larger quantities are called Pot-noodles. Usually soup noodles are served in individual bowls but pot noodles are served in a big pot in the centre of the table and individual diners fill their own bowls from the big pot. They are cooked more or less in the same way. Since a little of a large number of things is used, it is not very practical to make at home and, therefore, it is more a restaurant food. There are two kinds of fried noodles. One is the common fried noodles and the other is fried crispy noodles which is more difficult to prepare.

Mixed noodle types are the cold-gravy mixed and hot-gravy mixed noodles. The cold gravy mixed noodles are usually eaten in summer.

There are many varieties of raw noodles on sale in the market. They may be hand-swung, hand-cut, machine-cut, regular-dried, fined-dried or egg noodles. Besides all these, are rice flour noodles which are small, thin, easily broken and with a distinctive taste. They can be prepared as noodles and are sold in the market in dried form. The Chinese vermicelli or pea-starch noodles which is crisp, dry, transparent and hard to break when cooked, is very popular in soups and vegetable dishes and is not eaten as noodles. Peiping people are experts in making hand-swung noodles, a most difficult method of producing noodles. Machine-cut noodles are very common and can be as thin as 1/16 of an inch. The hand-cut noodles are easy to make in the home, but Chinese housewivies and chefs prefer to buy their noodles in the market either in the fresh or dried form. The general method of preparing the noodles before it is cooked in soup or fried is always the same. The following are some of the general methods employed:

Noodles

1. Bring 3 pints of water to the boil and put one pound of fresh noodles into it and boil about 3 minutes.
2. Use a pair of chopsticks or a fork to loose them in the boiling water so that the noodles will not stick to one another.
3. It takes about 3 minutes to boil the noodles. Then put them into cold water or cold boiled water and drain. Mix well with a little sesame oil or cooked oil; then loose them and lay them on a flat plate or tray before using.

If the raw noodles are steamed it is not necessary to rinse them in cold water. The proper way is to steam the noodles in a regular steamer for 10 minutes, mix with a little sesame oil and loose and lay on a flat tray. In case fresh noodles are not aviable in the market, the following recipes are given for dried noodles with the exception of one recipe for making hand-cut fresh noodles. If by chance fresh noodles are obtained, double the weight needed because fresh noodles are heavier in weight.

麵　條

Fresh Noodles

1 t-sp salt (or without)　　　2 eggs (optional)
1 lb. flour

Make a dough with 12 oz. flour, 2 eggs and salt. Knead well and roll out thinly. Roll the dough forward so that uneven rising of pastry may be avoided. Sprinkle some flour on the pastry-board and roll pastry evenly and frequently. Pleat the rolled pastry into 2 inch folds and cut crisply into very fine strips. Sprinkle a little flour over the strips and loosen them on a large plate or tray.

Fried Vegetarian Noodles

½ lb. noodles　　　　　　　　4 ozs. spinach
6 tb-sp cooking oil or　　　　1 t-sp salt
　duck fat　　　　　　　　　2 tb-sp soy sauce
½ lb. bamboo shoots　　　　½ tb-sp cornflour
10 mushrooms

Wash the spinach and if the leaves are small do not cut them. Wash the mushrooms and soak in ½ cup of hot water. Slice the bamboo shoots.

Noodles

Heat the oil and fry the bamboo shoots and mushrooms for 3 minutes. Add in the spinach and stir well with salt for 1 minute. Pour in the pre-cooked noodles and mix thoroughly for 2 minutes. Mix the cornflour with the soy sauce and mushroom water. Pour on the noodles and stir until the water thickens. Serve with pepper.

炒 麵

Fried Noodles

½ lb. noodles	2 slices ginger
½ lb. shrimps	1 tb-sp cornflour
4 mushrooms	½ tb-sp sherry (optional)
¼ lb. cabbage	4 tb-sp lard or cooking oil
¼ lb. bamboo shoots	1 t-sp salt
2 tb-sp soy sauce	½ t-sp sesame oil

Soak the mushrooms in hot water for 10 minutes. Cut off the stems and slice. Again cut the bamboo shoots and cabbage into slices. Shell the shrimps and wash them clean.

Put 1½ tb-sp lard in a frying pan and add the bamboo shoots first. Stir for 5 minutes then pour in the cabbage and ½ t-sp salt and cook for 3 minutes more. Remove from fire.

Mix the soy sauce, sherry, ginger and cornflour with the shelled shrimps. Heat 1tb-sp lard and fry the shrimps for 4 minutes. Pour in the cooked bamboo shoots and cabbage and stir for 1 more minute. Remove from fire.

Place the balance of the lard into the pan and pour in the pre-cooked noodles with 1½ t-sp salt. Turn the noodles from time to time for about 5 minutes. Add the cooked shrimps, cabbage, etc., stir over a big fire for 2 minutes. Serve immediately.

Some people prefer a dash of vinegar on the fried noodles.

Stewed Noodles

½ lb. noodles	1 tb-sp soy sauce
3 ozs. chicken meat	½ t-sp salt
5 mushrooms	1 oz. young leeks
2 cups of chicken soup	

Noodles

Prepare the noodles as usual and cook in the soup until soft or for about 1 minute. Soak the mushrooms in hot water and cut off the stems, add sliced chicken meat, young leeks, mushrooms, soy sauce and salt, then cook for another minute. Serve in noodle bowls with meat and vegetables on top.

炒 脆 麵

Fried Crispy Noodles

1 lb. noodles	1 tb-sp cornflour
½ lb. pork	½ tb-sp sherry (optional)
½ lb. shrimps	8 tb-sp lard
1 oz. mushrooms	½ tb-sp salt
¼ lb. spinach	2 tb-sp soy sauce
¼ lb. bamboo shoots	1 tb-sp sesame oil
1 egg (white)	

Steam the noodles for 10 minutes. Take them out and mix with the sesame oil. Allow them to become cold and separate them with a pair of chopsticks so that they don't stick together.

Soak the mushrooms in boiling water for 10 minutes. Cut off the stems and cut into slices. Shell and wash the shrimps. Peel off the skin of the bamboo shoots and cut them into slices also. Fry with 2 tb-sp lard for 5 minutes and add the spinach and salt. Stir constanly for 2 minutes then remove from fire. Mix the soy sauce, white of the egg, cornflour, sherry with the shelled shrimps and meat slices. Heat 2 tb-sp lard and fry the preparation about 4 minutes and mix in the cooked spinach and bamboo shoots. Remove from fire. Heat the remaining 4 tb-sp lard until hot and fry the noodles with salt. When the noodles are brown and crispy on both sides mix in the cooked ingredients for 2 minutes and serve.

For this recipe the noodles should preferably be steamed.

雞 湯 麵

Chicken Soup Noodles

½ lb. noodles	½ lb. chicken meat
2—3 spring onions	½ lb. ham
1½ pints chicken soup	2—3 slices ginger

Boil 1½ pints of water and put in the noodles after the water has started to boil. Boil for 5 more minutes. Pour off the water and rinse the noodles once with cold water.

Noodles

Boil the ham and chicken in the chicken soup. When well done cut them into shreds. Put the soaked and rinsed noodles in the hot soup and divide them into 6 bowls. Lay the ham and chicken shreds on the top of each bowl of noodles before serving. Mix the chopped ginger and spring onions with the noodles while eating if desired.

1 tb-sp soy sauce and 1 t-sp of lard may be added to the bowl, according to taste.

This is one of the simplest dishes to prepare and one which is as excellent as it is substantial.

雞 醬 麵
Soy Jam Noodles

½ lb. noodles	1 small cucumber.
1 cup soy jam	12 radishes
3 tb-sp cooking oil or lard	½ lb. pea sprouts
1 t-sp chopped ginger	7—8 spring onions

Mince the pork and mix half of the spring onions which have been chopped fine—the green portion should be used as well as the white. Chop the ginger root very fine until the equivalent of one teaspoonful is obtained. Mix these ingredients thoroughly. Heat the vegetable oil in a frying pan and add the above mixture. Fry for 5 minutes stirring the mixture constantly. Add the cup of soy jam while stirring and then add one cup of water, a little at a time, continuing to stir the mixture while cooking for about 10 minutes.

The remaining spring onions should be chopped very fine. The radishes should be peeled and sliced lengthwise, very thin. The pea sprouts should be immersed in boiling water for about 2 minutes. Place all these accompaniments on separate dishes and put on the dining table. The noodles should be prepared in the usual way. Serve the noodles in individual bowls. Each person should help himself to 1 tb-sp soy jam and also a little of each of the accompaniments. Mix them well before eating.

Pastry and Sweet Dishes

點 心 與 麵 食

Chapter 12. Pastry And Sweet Dishes

With the exception of steamed bread, fancy rolls are eaten as part of the ordinary food. Both pastry and sweet dishes are eaten as refreshments in China. They are also served at intervals in banquets to break up the monotony of dinner courses. Sweet dishes are usually a make-up combination of things which are served as a course at banquets. Sweet refreshments are mostly pastry with sweet stuffing. Pastry is sometimes plain or salty, or may be fried, steamed or boiled.

In view of the limitation of ingredients in foreign countries the following recipes are limited to include materials which are more easily available.

饅 頭

Steamed Bread or *Man-T'ou*

5 cups flour   1 cake fresh yeast
                           1 tb-sp diluted alkali

Dissolve the yeast in 2 cups of lukewarm water which will be used to knead the flour into dough. If the flour is very dry use a little more water. The dough should be placed in a heavy pot in a warm place; cover the dough with a damp towel to keep the surface from getting to dry. After about 4 hours, the dough will have grown to about 4 times its original size with a lot of holes inside. In winter put the dough for raising in a slightly warmed oven or over the pilot light of a gas stove. Add diluted alkali and knead well.

Use ½ cup of flour as dusting flour. Take out the dough and knead it and divide into 20 portions equally. Use the thumbs and index fingers to work each piece like a half ball with a bottom. Another style is to have the roll stand up high like a rounded haystack. To get this shape squeeze and roll gently and repeatedly between palms and make a bottom to stand on the steamer. Put them aside for they may have a second raising. After 10 minutes arrange them on a steam tier and steam for 10 minutes.

When they are understeamed, under-raised or anything has gone wrong, dark unraised sports and uncooked parts may result. If they are steamed right, they will be always good for reheating.

Pastry and Sweet Dishes

飽 子
Steamed Stuffed Bread Or *Pao-Tzu*

Pao-tzu is a kind of stuffed steamed bread which is usually eaten at breakfast or as between meal and refreshments. The making of the bread part is the same as *Man-t'ou* which is unstuffed and serves very often as the main part of a meal with accompanied dishes.

After the dough is made as usual, divide into 20 parts and roll them with a rolling pin into a round shape about 3 inches across.

Pao—Tzu

1. *Salty stuffings:*
   2 lbs. ground pork
   2 tb-sp soy sauce
   1 tb-sp sesame oil
      or salad oil
   1 t-sp sugar
   2 t-sp salt
   1 spring onion

Mix thoroughly the minced pork and all the seasonings. Place one of the prepared pieces of dough on the palm of the left hand and put a portion, 1—2 tb-sp of the stuffing in its centre. With the fingers of the right hand, turn up the rim bit by bit to warp around the stuffing until only a small opening is left at the top centre. Close this top by pinching the edges together.

Steam in the same way as in recipe *Man-t'ou*.

There are many kinds of stuffing. Substitution of shrimps, for one-third of the meat; substitution of mutton for pork, with the addition of few pieces of chopped ginger and one or two pieces of spring onion. Crab-meat, red-braised meat, roast pork, chicken may also be used as stuffing. Among all crab-meat stuffed *Pao-tzu* is the best. Vegetable stuffing may also be used; spinach and leek are very frequently used, in which case more sesame oil will be needed.

2. *Sweet stuffings:*
   1 cup almonds
   1 cup walnuts
   1 cup sesame seeds
   ½ cup sugar
   4 dozen kernels of water
      melon seeds
   1 tb-sp lard

Pastry and Sweet Dishes

Grind the almonds and walnuts very fine; then roast in frying pan over a medium fire for 1 or 2 minutes. Mix the ground ingredients with the lard and divide into 20 portions. Do the same thing to stuff the pieces of dough and steam in the same way.

It is the usual practice to steam the sweet and salty stuffed *Pao-tzu* in the same steamer but it is usual to differentiate them by marking each of the sweet stuffed *Pao-tzu* with a red dot on the centre at the top.

餛　飩

Rambling Or *Hun-T'un*

60—70 sheets of *Hun-t'un* skin	1 tb-sp sesame oil or salad oil
1 lb. pork	½ t-sp salt
4 tb-sp soy sauce	1 spring onion
	6 cups of stock

Mince the meat and mix with 2 tb-sp soy sauce, oil, salt, and chopped spring onion. Put ½ t-sp of the stuffing on the centre of each skin. Gather and pinch lightly where it meets again after wrapping around the meat, leaving the edges to ramble freely.

Boil 12 cups of water over a big fire and drop the *Hun-t'un* in to boil. Remove from fire and drain. Put 1 tb-sp of soy sauce in each rice bowl and put the boiled *Hun-t'un* and hot stock in the bowls. Serve with pepper and dip the *Hun-t'un* in soy sauce to suit taste.

In China, the *Hun-t'un* skin is always found ready made in market. If such skin is not available in Western Markets, it can be made at home.

The Preparation of the Pastry.

1 lb. flour	1 t-sp salt
2 eggs	1 tb-sp diluted alkali or lye

Sift the flour and salt. Make a hole in centre and pour in the beaten eggs and diluted alkali. Mix well and make a soft dough. Roll on the flour board until it is as thin as paper. Cut into 2 inch square.

Pastry and Sweet Dishes

餃 子

Meat Dumpling Or *Chiao-Tzu*

Chiao-tzu is a form of meat dumpling—a core of meat and vegetable or meat only surrounded by a light thin paste which is smaller and thicker than the skin or wrapping of Spring Rolls. It may be either boiled or steamed, and the filling used can be varied according to individual taste.

Its preparation is divided into two parts.

1. The Preparation of the Dough:

½ t-sp salt   2 cups flour

Measure 2 cups of sifted flour and salt into a bowl and add enough warm water, mix them thoroughly with a spoon or a pair of chopsticks until they turn into a very light dough. Avoid dryness by covering with a damp cloth before proceeding with the composition of the filling mixture.

2. The Preparation of the filling:

1 lb. pork	6 spring onions
2 t-sp olive oil or sesame oil	1 cup soy sauce
	1 lb. cabbage
¼ lb. leeks	1 t-sp salt
3 slices ginger	

Chop or mince the meat and spring onions, the white part should be ground as well as the green. Chop a small piece of ginger very finely until the equivalent of ½ t-sp has been obtained and mix 1 t-sp of soy sauce, salt, sesame oil or substitutes and the chopped cabbage with the meat. The white portions of the leeks should also be chopped very fine and added to the mixture. Mix all the ingredients thoroughly.

Flour a rolling pin and board as one would for biscuits. Knead a small quantity of flour into a dough until it is quite dry but still pastic. Roll into a long thin string, resembling a snake about 1 inch in diameter. Pinch off uniformly small pieces about an inch long. Press with the rolling pin and make into small flat cakes. Roll very thin but try to maintain

Pastry and Sweet Dishes

uniform circular shapes 3 inches in diameter. Place a heaped teaspoonful of the filling mixture on each cake, fold it over once and press the edge together by pinching quickly with the forefinger and thumb. The shape is just like a half moon.

Heat about 4 bowls of water in a boiler. When boiling starts, drop with care ten or fifteen *Chiao-tzu* into it and boil for 8 to 15 minutes; use a perforated spoon or ladle to remove them when they are floating.

It is customary to immerse or dip *Chiao-tzu* into two condiments, vinegar and soy sauce, or one according to the individual taste, before eating. In case there is any left-over, they may be kept and heated up again the next day or be fried till golden brown. They are not good to eat if they are cold.

There are many ways of preparing the stuffing. Here is another of them:

4 oz. bamboo shoots	2 spring onions
1 lb. spinach	4 tb-sp soy sauce
2 t-sp salt	8 tb-sp lard
2 slices flour	1 lb. pork

The pork should be medium fat and minced with spinach, bamboo shoots, onions and ginger. Mix well with soy sauce, salt and lard. Put the minced pork and well mixed stuffings in the middle of the round paste and fold it as a half moon shape as in the foregoing direction. Same method of cooking is also to be employed.

Patties

The preparations of the Patties are divided into 2 parts:

1. *The pastry*—the first part of the preparation:

1 lb. flour	1 t-sp salt
1 egg	

Make a pastry with 1 lb. flour, 1 egg, 1 cupful of water and 1 t-sp salt. The water should not be added all at once, but should be mixed in as quickly as possible. Roll out thinly and cut into rounds about 3 inches in diameter. In order to avoid uneven rising of the pastry, rolling should always be done forwards.

Pastry and Sweet Dishes

2. *The stuffing*—the second part of the preparation:

1 lb. pork	1 t-sp sherry (optional)
½ lb. leeks or cabbage	1 lb. lard or cooking oil
1 tb-sp soy sauce	½ t-sp salt

Chop or mince the meat with ½ lb. cabbage or leeks, fry in 2 tb-sp lard or cooking oil for 10 minutes and season with the soy sauce and cooking sherry. Let it get cold then divide evenly as many as half the number of the pastry.

There are also three methods in cooking the patties:

1. The first method is to take a round and put 1 tb-sp or more of the stuffing in the centre and take another to cover it up. Close the edge tightly with a little cold water and press around with fingers. Fry in deep oil until crisp and brown and serve with vinegar and soy sauce.

2. The second is to fry the patties in 4 tb-sp oil or lard until the bottom of each one is brown. Pour ½ cupful of soup or water over the patties and cook them for 3 minutes with lid covered tightly. When the steam has penetrated into the part of the patties and the water in the pan has evaporated, they will be ready for serving with vinegar and soy sauce. This method is more economical when oil or lard is not plentiful.

3. The third method is to steam the patties in a large tightly covered steamer at a moderate heat for half an hour.

The patties are good to eat with congee and are the favourite pastry of the northern people of China.

春 捲

Spring Rolls

Spring Rolls are eaten during spring or after the Chinese New Year. They are fried stuffed rolls of very thin dough which is not raised. The skin or wrapping is made from baking a thin paste of wheat flour which makes the skin more crisp and lighter after being fried than that made if such skin is not available in Western markets, it can be made from wheat flour at home.

Spring Rolls

Pastry and Sweet Dishes

The preparation of the Spring Rolls may be divided into two parts.

1. The preparation of the skin. Make a mixture with ½ lb. flour, 1 t-sp salt and 1½ cups of water or more. Heat a small frying pan, about 6 inches diameter, on a very low heat, grease its surface evenly with a piece of oil-soak cloth and pour a tablespoonful of flour mixture into the frying pan. Let it run evenly over the whole pan until dry, then turn it on a flat plate. Repeat the same process until the mixture is finished.

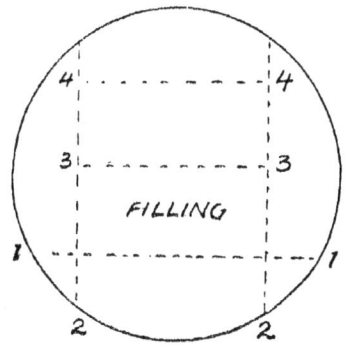

How to wrap the Spring Roll

2. The ingredients of stuffing:

½ lb. pork	1 t-sp salt
½ lb. pea sprouts	1 tb-sp soy sauce
½ lb. fresh shrimps	5 tb-sp lard
7—8 spring onions	1 lb. cooking oil

Wash the pea sprouts, cut the pork and spring onions into shreds. Shell the shrimps. Heat the lard over a big fire and fry the pork and shrimps for 1 minute. Then add the spring onion and pea sprouts and fry for 3 minutes. During the process of frying, pour in the soy sauce and salt. Leave the cooked meat and vegetables in a cool place for at least half an hour.

Heap the cooked meat and vegetables oblong-wise in the centre of the pastry, fold up both ends first, then the sides. Close the edges with a little water. Divide the stuffing equally as the number of the skin. Heat the oil till hot, turn to low fire if it has a tendency to smoke. Fry 3 or 4 at a time until they are brown. Bring the oil to the boiling before the second lot is fried.

Pastry and Sweet Dishes

葱 油 餅
Fried Spring Onion Cake

1 tb-sp salt	4 zo. spring onions
4 cups flour	½ lb. lard

Chop the spring onions. Knead the flour with 2 cups of water into a soft dough and then divide into 12 portions. Roll each portion with a rolling pin into a cake of about ½ foot in diameter. Then spread 2 tb-sp of chopped spring onion, 1 tb-sp lard or vegetable oil and ¼ t-sp salt over each cake. Roll up each cake and then twist into a standing screw. Use the rolling pin to flatten the screw from top to bottom into a cake of about 3 inches in diameter.

Heat 1 tb-sp of lard or vegetable oil in a deep frying pan. Put in the cake, and fry each side over a medium fire for 2 minutes. Turn to a low fire and fry for 3 minutes on each side, that is altogether about 10 minutes for each cake until the outside of the cake has turned brown and crisp but the inside is stil soft. Cut each cake into six to eight portions and serve hot with hot soup, congee or millet congee, if obtainable, which will make a hearty meal and take away one's hungry feeling all at once.

花 捲
Steam Fancy Rolls

5 cups flour	1 t-sp salt
1 cake fresh yeast	2 t-sp vegetable oil
	1 tb-sp diluted alkali

Fancy Roll

Dissolve the yeast in 2 cups of lukewarm and add to it the flour a little at a time. Knead the flour into dough then let it stand and raise for about 4 hours. Place it in a warm oven if the weather is cold. When raised take out and knead down the dough. Add the alkali. Divide the dough into halves and roll each half into a flat piece 12—15 inches across. Use about 2 tb-sp or more dusting flour to prevent sticking during the process of rolling.

Pastry and Sweet Dishes

Rub ½ t-sp salt and 2 t-sp oil on the surface of each piece and roll it up like a carpet. Thus the dough is slightly lengthened. Cut into 10 or 12 equal sections. Press one-third the way down on the middle of each section, with a chopstick or the back of a Chinese cleaver paralled with the orginal cutting. This is called a Fancy Roll. Put aside about 10 minutes and steam as usual. Both *Man-t'ou* and Fancy Rolls make perfect complements to braised meat with soy sauce.

白 木 耳 湯

White Fungis Soup

2 tb-sp white fungus   1 oz. rock sugar

Soak the white fungus in water and wash away all the sand and black stuff, if any. Put in a big bowl with water and steam on a low fire for 1 hour. Then add in the rock sugar and keep steaming for another 1 hour. It is ready to serve when the fungus becomes soft and transparent.

It is often served at a feast as a dessert and is considered an elegant dish. It is also said that the dish is very nourishing and nutritious for invalids and old people who should take it every day. White fungus of the best quality is very white and without much black stuff and sand; the inferior quality is yellowish and a lot of time has to be spent in washing it. Again the best quality fungus becomes much bigger after it is soaked in water.

豆 腐 漿

Soy Bean Milk

1 cup soy bean   3 pints water

Wash the soy beans and soak overnight. Grind the soy beans, adding the 3 pints of water gradually during the process of grinding. Boil the milk and drain away the refuse. Heat the milk again after draining and add sugar and serve.

A little almond essence or other flavour can be added to make the milk more tasty. It can be drunk either cold or hot. It is very nutritious.

南 瓜 丸

Fried Pumpkin Balls

1 pumpkin (3 lbs.)   ½ lb. fresh lard
2 cups glutinous rice powder   1½ ozs. sugar

Pastry and Sweet Dishes

Peel the pumpkin and cut into thin slices. Put them into a boiler and boil with the rice bowls of water until they are very soft. Mash them and mix with the glutinous powder and sugar.

Cut the fresh lard in dices; then make the mashed pumpkin into small balls each about as big as an egg. Again make a hole in the centre, put the diced lard in the centre of the ball and as much as it can hold then close it up by pressing the edges together. Do the same thing until the mushed pumpkin is finished. Arrange them on a perforated partition but if this cannot be done arrange them in a big bowl, and steam for ½ hour.

Pumpkin balls can be fried if desired. Heat about ½ lb. vegetable oil till hot and fry them until brown. Most people prefer fried to steamed balls because the smell is more fragrant.

炸 山 芋

Fried Sweet Potatoes

1 lb. sweet potatoes ½ cup syrup
½ lb. vegetable oil

Put the syrup in a bowl and steam for 10 minutes after the water in the boiler has started boiling. Do not remove from the boiler or allow it to get cold.

Peel off the skin of the sweet potatoes, then cut them into thin slices. Wash them and drain off the extra moisture. Heat the oil till smoking and fry the potatoes until each piece turns golden brown. Remove from fire and place them on a serving plate. Pour the hot syrup on top and serve hot.

蓮 子 糯 米 粥

Lotus Seed And Glutinous Rice Congee

1 cup glutinous rice 3 ozs. sugar
½ cup dry lotus seeds

Soak the lotus seeds in hot water. Remove the outer skin. Use a toothpick or match stick to insert into the end of the seed to push out the heart of the seed. The heart is green in colour and taste bitter so always

Pastry and Sweet Dishes

remove it before cooking. Wash the seeds again and put them in a boiler with 3 pints of water. Keep boiling for 1 hour over a low fire until only about 2 pints of water are left.

Wash the glutinous rice and put it into the same boiler to boil together with the lotus seeds until the rice is soft and forms a gelatin mass. Mix in the rock sugar and serve either hot or cold.

八 寶 飯

Eight Precious Rice

1 lb. glutinous rice	Assorted honey preserved fruit
¼ lb. lard	
¼ cup sugar	

Soak the glutinous rice over night. Put in a big bowl and steam in a boiler with ½ cup of water until it is soft. Mix in the lard and sugar, then at the bottom of a large bowl arrange honey preserved fruits of various kind such as lotus seeds, dates, raisins, cherry, etc., a little of each kind to make a colourful pattern. Carefully pour the rice on top. Put the bowl into the steamer and steam for two more hours until the rice is very soft. Take the bowl out, hold the top of a large plate against the glutinous rice, invert both plate and bowl in one decisive movement. In such a way, the bowl can be removed and the rice with the fruit design will be shown on top of the plate. Serve hot.

This dish is extraordinarily hot so when it is served right after cooking, special care must be taken while eating it.

Sweet and Sour Dishes

雜　類

Chapter 13.　Specialities

糖　醋　類

Sweet And Sour Dishes

The widely known "Sweet and Sour" dishes prepared by Chinese are particularly favoured by foreign residents in the country. Certain meats and vegetables are prepared in the same manner, but fish, when prepared with the so-called sweet and sour sauce is exceptionally appetising. The sauce is made with the vinegar and sugar and its flavour has much in common with the oil and vinegar French salad dressing. There are a number of variations of the sauce, according to the districts of China. Some sauce is prepared more sour than others, it usually differs according to individual taste. The sauce is sometimes prepared with pork, fish or vegetables but sometimes separately as shown in the following recipes.

Regarding the vinegar sold in the market, there are different varieties of sourness, therefore, one extra tb-sp of vinegar may be added to the recipe if desired.

糖　醋　汁

Sweet And Sour Sauce

4 tb-sp cornflour　　　　　　　2 tb-sp vinegar
2 tb-sp sugar　　　　　　　　　3 tb-sp tomato sauce
1 tb-sp soy sauce　　　　　　　1 t-sp salt.

Mix the cornflour with 2 cups of water, vinegar, soy sauce and sugar in a saucepan. Stir well over a low fire until boiling then mix with the tomato sauce. This is the basic sweet-sour sauce which can be applied to most of the sweet and sour dishes in case they are prepared separately. One tablespoon of tomato sauce makes the sweet and sour sauce a little more colourful. The idea of using tomato sauce in our Chinese cooking comes from our Western friends. In the old days, tomato sauce was not used in cooking but nowadays, the leading Cantonese restaurants in Shanghai use **tomato sauce freely.**

Sweet and Sour Dishes

糖 醋 肉
Sweet And Sour Pork

1 lb. pork
1 green pepper
4 tb-sp flour
1 tomato
1 egg

1 small carrot
1 lb. cooking oil
1 small cucumber
1 t-sp salt

Cut the green pepper, tomato, carrots and cucumber into triangular pieces. Chop pork into the same size though not in the same shape. Whip the egg and mix with flour and ½ t-sp salt. Drop the pieces into it and mix well. Heat the fat until boiling and fry each piece of pork until it is brown and; drain well.

Each lot of frying must be done when the oil is boiling otherwise the pork will not be crisp. Leave only a tablespoon of oil in the pan and pour in the green pepper, tomato, carrot and cucumber. Add the remaining ½ t-sp salt and stir for 1 minute and mix with the fried pork. Heat the sweet and sour sauce and pour on top of the pork. Remove from pan and serve hot.

This dish can be prepared a few hours before serving but mix the fried pork with the sauce only on eating. When it is time to serve the meal, heat the frying oil again and put in the pork for 1 minute and also reheat the sauce, Chinese food always tastes better when hot.

糖 醋 荔 枝 肉
Sweet And Sour Pork With Lichee

Use same method and ingredients as the preceding recipe. Add one can of preserved Lichee. If desired, green peppers and tomatoes may be omitted.

糖 醋 肉 丸
Sweet And Sour Pork Balls

1 lb. pork
¼ cup soy sauce (light)
2 tb-sp sherry (optional)
2 eggs
1 t-sp sugar

1 t-sp black pepper
2 tb-sp flour
½ spring onion
1 lb. cooking oil

Sweet and Sour Dishes

With a sharp cleaver and chopping board chop the fresh meat. This is preferable to putting it through a grinder. Chop the spring onion very fine and add to the mixture, soy sauce, salt, sherry, sugar, flour, 2 eggs and ½ cup of water.

Between the palms make balls, smaller than an egg. Heat the cooking oil to the proper temperature for deep-frying and fry the meat balls till brown and crispy. Remove, drain off the oil and place on a serving dish, pour the sweet and sour sauce on top of the fried balls and serve. If desired, sectioned spring onion and red pepper shreds can be added to the sauce to make the dish look more delicious.

糖 醋 魚 丸

Sweet And Sour Fish Balls

1½ fish
1 slice ginger
1 t-sp pepper
2 t-sp cornflour
½ t-sp salt

Remove the head of the fish, then split it from the back into 2 halves. With a spoon, scrape the inside of the fish from the tail toward the head. Do not scrape in the reverse direction as then the fine bones will turn loose and the meat cannot be scraped out. Chop the fish finely. Dissolve the salt in a cup of water and add it gradually to the meat. Add the pepper and cornflour and mix them thoroughly again, then take a fistful of the seasoned fish and squeeze it out through the hole formed by the index finger and the thumb and scoop with a spoon.

In this way fish balls will be formed. Put them into hot water and boil them for 3 minutes. They can be stored in a refrigerator for days. Fried in deep oil until brown and served with a sweet and sour sauce and pickles.

糖 醋 龍 蝦

Sweet And Sour Lobster

1 lb. cooked lobster meat
2 eggs
3/4 cup flour
1 tb-sp lemon juice
1 t-sp soy sauce
½ t-sp pepper
1 lb. cooking oil
½ t-sp chopped ginger
1 t-sp salt

Sweet and Sour Dishes

Mix the lemon juice, chopped ginger and soy sauce together; pour over the cooked lobster and soak for 5 minutes. Beat up the flour and eggs to form a smooth paste; add salt and pepper. Dip soaked lobster in egg batter and fry in the hot oil until golden brown. Put in a deep plate. Heat the sweet and sour sauce and pour on top of the fried lobster and serve hot.

糖 醋 菠 蘿 龍 蝦

Sweet And Sour Lobster With Pineapple

Follow the preceding recipe, adding 1½ cups sliced pineapple to the sauce.

糖 醋 荔 枝 龍 蝦

Sweet And Sour Lobster with Lichee

Follow the same recipe, adding 1 can of preserved lichee to the sauce.

糖 醋 哈 唎

Sweet And Sour Clams

Use same method and ingredients as the sweet and sour lobster using shelled clams instead of lobster. (Steam the clams first.)

糖 醋 魚

Sweet And Sour Fish

1 fish (3 lbs.)	1 egg
6 tb-sp flour	1 tb-sp salt
1 tb-sp sherry (optional)	1 lb. cooking oil
1 spring onion	3—4 slices ginger

Mandarin, perch, carp and mullet make the best sweet and sour fish. Clean the fish and slash the back with a few incisions. Mix the beaten egg with flour and a little water. Rub the salt and sherry evenly on both the inside and outside of the fish, do the same with the flour batter.

Heat the oil until hot and fry the fish for about 10 to 14 minutes until brown and crisp. Pour off the oil leaving only 1 tablespoonful. Put in the sectioned spring onion, ginger and the sweet and sour sauce, and pour on top of the fish. If desired, red pepper shreds or sweet pickle shreds can be added to the sauce to make the fish more colourful.

Sweet and Sour Dishes

糖 醋 蝦
Sweet And Sour Shrimp

Use same method and ingredients as in the recipe for sweet and sour lobster using shrimps instead of lobsters.

糖 醋 蝦 球
Sweet And Sour Shrimp Balls

2 lbs. shrimps	1 egg
½ lb. pork	1 t-sp salt
2 tb-sp flour	2 tb-sp soy sauce
1 t-sp sherry (optional)	8 tb-sp cooking oil

Mince the pork and shrimps after they are washed and shelled thoroughly. Add beaten egg, flour, sherry, salt and soy sauce to the ground pork and shrimps. Make the paste into pigeon egg size balls.

Heat the oil till hot and fry both sides of the balls on a medium fire until they are light brown. Never use a big fire which will make them burn outside and leave them raw inside. Pour the sweet and sour sauce on top and serve.

糖 醋 雞
Sweet And Sour Chicken

1 lb. chicken meat	2 cups mixed sweet pickles
1 t-sp soy sauce (light)	
¼ t-sp salt	2 eggs
½ cup flour	½ lb cooking oil

Beat the eggs and mix with flour to form a smooth paste. Soak the chicken cubes in the soy sauce and salt for 10 to 15 minutes. Dip in the batter and fry in deep oil until golden brown. Pour the sweet and sour sauce with the sliced sweet pickles and serve.

糖 醋 雞 球
Sweet And Sour Chicken Balls

1 spring chicken	1 small onion
1 t-sp salt	½ lb. cooking oil
1 tb-sp cornflour	1 t-sp sugar

Remove the skin of the chicken and take off all the bones with a cleaver or knife. Mince the meat and chop the spring onion into small section, then mix them together. Add the salt, cornflour, and about 2 tb-sp of water and again mix them thoroughly. Use the plams to make them into small balls approximately about the size of pigeon eggs.

Sweet and Sour Dishes

Heat the lard till hot, put the seasoned chicken balls in and fry them until golden brown. Pour the sweet and sour sauce with sectioned spring onion and red pepper shreds and serve hot.

糖 醋 江 芽 柱
Sweet And Sour Scallops

Use same method and ingredients as in sweet and sour lobster, using scallops instead of lobsters.

糖 醋 魷 魚
Sweet And Sour Fresh Squid

Same as the preceding recipe, using fresh squid.

糖 醋 鱔 魚
Sweet And Sour Eel

4 tb-sp cooking oil	1 tb-sp sherry (optional)
1 t-sp salt	1 t-sp ginger (crushed)
1 clove garlic	¼ lb. bacon
1½—2 lbs. eels	½ t-sp pepper
2 t-sp soy sauce (light)	¼ t-sp sesame oil
6 mushrooms	1 tb-sp leek (chopped)
¼ cup water chestnuts	3 cups soup
1 bamboo shoot	

Kill the eels and boil them with 2 or 3 slices of ginger for 20 to 25 minutes. Rinse in cold water, remove the bones and cut into sections about 1½ inches. Soak the mushrooms in warm water and cut into shreds. Remove the outer skin of the bamboo shoot and water chestnuts and shred them. Mix soy sauce, sherry, 1 t-sp chopped ginger, ½ t-sp sesame oil, ½ t-sp pepper and 1 tb-sp water, stir well.

Put the oil in the skillet, add salt and crushed garlic. Pour in the sectioned eel and fry on both sides until light brown. Add the prepared mixture, cover and cook for ½ minute. Add bacon shreds, mushroom shreds, water chestnuts, bamboo shoots and chopped leeks. Then add the soup and cook until boiling. Lower the heat and simmer until water is almost gone. (about ½ cup soup left.) Pour on the sweet and sour sauce and serve.

All dishes can be prepared a few hours before serving but mix the fried pork, fish, lobster, etc., with the sauce only on eating. When it is time

Sweet and Sour Dishes

to serve the meal, heat the frying oil again and fry for 1 minute and also reheat the sauce, sweet and sour food always taste better when hot.

The following recipes are prepared with the Sweet and Sour Sauce.

糖 醋 皮 蛋
Sweet And Sour 100-Year-Old Egg

6 100-year-old eggs ½ t-sp salt
4 tb-sp lard

Remove the outside coating and shell the egg. Cut egg into four portions. Heat the fat and fry the eggs for 1 minute and add the salt. Then pour in the mixture of 1 tb-sp vinegar, 1 tb-sp sugar, 1 tb-sp soy sauce, 2 tb-sp of cornflour and 1 cup of water and stir until the mixture becomes translucent.

The Europeans and Americans have long believed that the curious eggs encased in unsavoury mud, seen in Chinese shops, are at least one hundred years old and have been named accordingly. They are not, of course, a hundred years old or anything like it. They are also known as "Ming Dynasty Eggs." Both names are given because they seen to be very old but that is incorrect. It is true however that they are good when they are hundred days old. Their Mandarin name is "*Pee-tan.*"

The eggs themselves are duck eggs enclosed in a coat of mud, lime and wheat, which leads to a chemical and physical change of the yolk of the egg, giving it a distinctive flavour. It is not true that they can be kept for many years. The eggs can be bought in most Chinese provision shops.

糖 醋 海 螺
Sweet And Sour Conch

4 conches (large size)	2 tomatoes
1 t-sp soy sauce (light)	1 cup mixed sweet pickles
1 t-sp sherry	
1 t-sp chopped ginger	2 pepper
¼ t-sp sesame oil	2 eggs
1½ tb-sp soy sauce (black)	¼ t-sp pepper
1 tb-sp cornflour	¼ t-sp salt
½ cup sugar	⅓ cup vinegar
¾ cup flour	½ lb. cooking oil

Sweet and Sour Dishes

Remove the shells from the conches. Wash with hot water then boil first adding 2 tb-sp baking powder to water, for 1 hour or until tender.

Cut into cubes, mix soy sauce (light), sherry, chopped ginger, and sesame oil together; add 1 tb-sp water. Stir well. Beat the eggs and flour vigorously until a smooth paste is formed. Add pepper and salt and mix well. Mix the black soy sauce with cornflour and ½ cup of water and stir well. Soak the conches in the sesame oil preparation for 15 minutes or more. Dip in egg mixture, fry in deep fat until golden brown. Place in a deep plate. Pour 1 cup water into hot skillet, add vinegar and sugar. Add diced tomatoes, peppers and mixed sweet pickles. Pour in the cornflour preparation gradually and stir constantly until sauce thickens and is smooth; pour over conch and serve. Garnish with Chinese parsley.

糖 醋 菠 蘿 海

Sweet And Sour Conch With Pineapple

Use same method and ingredients as the preceding recipe, adding 2 cups diced pineapple to the sauce.

糖 醋 魚 片

Sweet And Sour Fish Slices

1 fish (about 2 lbs.)	2 tb-sp sugar
¼ cup vinegar	½ cup sherry (optional)
1 tb-sp cornflour	¼ cup soy sauce
½ t-sp salt	¼ lb. cooking oil
2 spring onions	2 red peppers

Carefully clean and cut the fish into big slices. Season with salt and fry in hot oil until good and brown on both sides and then remove the fish to a warm platter while the following sauce is being prepared.

In the pan in which the fish has been fried leave about 2 tb-sp of oil and put the vinegar, wine, sugar, the soy sauce, cornflour and ½ cup of water. As soon as the sauce shows signs of thickening pour it over the fish. Garnish with sectioned spring onion and red pepper shreds which are merely for decoration. Serve immediately after cooking.

Sweet and Sour Dishes

糖 醋 排 骨
Sweet And Sour Ribs

1 lb. pork spare ribs	½ cup sugar
1 lb. cooking oil	¼ cup soy sauce
2 tb-sp sherry (optional)	1 t-sp salt
2 cups cornflour	½ t-sp minced ginger
2 tb-sp vinegar	

With a sharp, heavy cleaver cut the spare ribs into pieces approximately 1 inch long and as wide as the rib happens to be. Wash in cold water and drain well. Dip immediately into the cornflour and fry in cooking oil until a golden brown and remove quickly. Drain the oil from the pan with the exception of two tablespoonfuls, replace the spare ribs and add the vinegar, the minced ginger-root, sugar, salt, sherry, soy sauce and 1 cup of water which has been mixed with 2 tb-sp cornflour. Serve when the mixture shows signs of thickening.

糖 醋 白 菜
Sweet And Sour Cabbage

1 lb. cabbage	1 tb-sp soy sauce
3 tb-sp cooking oil or lard	2 tb-sp cornflour
	1½ tb-sp sugar
½ t-sp salt	1 tb-sp vinegar

Wash the cabbage and cut it into pieces about 1 inch square. Heat the oil till hot; then put the cabbage into the frying pan. Stir for 1 minute, add the salt and half cup of water. Cover the pan and cook for 10 minutes. While cooking stir occasionally.

Mix the vinegar, sugar, cornflour, and soy sauce with 1 cup of water. When the cabbage is done pour in the mixture and stir till the juice becomes translucent.

糖 醋 胡 菠 蘿
Sweet And Sour Carrots

10 small carrots	1½ tb-sp sugar
2 tb-sp cooking oil or lard	1 tb-sp vinegar
	1 tb-sp cornflour
½ t-sp salt	1 tb-sp soy sauce
6 mustard green	4 tb-sp lard

Sweet and Sour Dishes

Wash the carrots but do not peel them Cut into slices. Heat the lard and fry the carrots for 1 minute; then add salt and half a cup of water. Boil for 5 minutes. If the carrots are big and old, cook a little longer.

Mix the vinegar, sugar, soy sauce, cornflour and 1 cup of water. Add the mixture to the carrots and cook until the gravy is translucent.

糖 醋 芥 菜

Sweet And Sour Mustard Green

½ lb. mustard green
2 tb-sp cornflour
2 tb-sp cornflour
1 tb-sp soy sauce

1½ tb-sp vinegar
3 tb-sp lard
½ t-sp salt

Mix the vinegar and sugar with ½ cup of water and the cornflour with another cup of water. Stir well before using. Cut the mustard green into sections and squeeze dry, fry in the lard for 10 minutes until very dry then add the vinegar mixture and stir for 2 minutes. Add cornflour preparation and stir until gravy is thick and translucent.

Birds' Nest

燕　窩

Birds' Nests

The birds' nests from which the traditional Chinese dishes are made are built by a certain kind of swallow living round the coasts of the China Sea. These birds eat small fishes, and build their nests from saliva which dries in the sun and is flavoured by the fish.

Chinese gourmets say the best edible birds' nests come from the Philippines, although there are many other sources. In Malaya they often come from certain parts of North Borneo.

There are two kinds of edible nests, hairy or plain. The nests are about the size of a large soup spoon, and when soaked in water any adherent matter cleaned away, they separate into shreds.

Prices vary considerably with the quality of the nests and the supply situation. A Chinese cook will probably get better nests for less money than if you go shopping for them yourself.

The preliminary treatment of the nests is the same for all dishes. Soak them in hot water, periodically renewing it, for at least 6 hours. Pick off all hair, dirt or adherent matter and steam the nests for 2 hours.

雞　肉　燕　窩

Birds' Nests With Minced Chicken

1 oz. birds' nest (weighed before steaming)	1 slice of ham
2 oz. fresh or cooked chicken	3 cups soup (chicken or meat)
	2 t-sp salt

Simmer the nests in a saucepan with the soup for 15 minutes then add the chopped chicken, ham and salt. Heat until boiling. If it is not immediately served, keep it in the refrigerator and warm before serving.

Two egg whites, and 1 t-sp of cornflour mixed with water may be added if a thicker soup is preferred.

Birds' Nest

奶 油 燕 窩

Birds' Nests With Cream Soup

1 oz. birds' nest
1 t-sp cornflour
2 slices of ham
2 t-sp salt

1½ pints stock (chicken or meat)
1 cup evaporated milk

Soak and steam the birds' nests as described above. Put the milk mixed with the cornflour into the chicken soup and heat on a low fire, stirring well until boiling. Pour in the already softened birds' nest, chopped ham and salt and allow to simmer for another 5 minutes. Serve hot.

杏 仁 燕 窩 羹

Birds' Nests With Almond Soup

2 cups almond
1 oz. birds' nest

¼ cup rock sugar or sugar
2 cups almond

Prepare the birds' nest as above. Soak the almonds in hot water and remove the skin. Grind the almonds very finely. Boil with the 1½ pints of water and strain with a piece of gauze. Add the rock sugar and the birds' nest to the strained almond milk, heat until boiling. Serve either cold or hot.

鴿 蛋 燕 窩 湯

Pigeon Eggs And Birds' Nests Soup

1 oz. birds' nest
1 doz. pigeon eggs

1 big bowl of soup
1 t-sp salt

Prepare the birds' nest as usual. Boil and shell the pigeon eggs. Steam the birds' nests with eggs in the soup for 20 minutes. Add salt and serve.

Shark's Fins

魚 翅

Shark's Fins

A dish of shark's fins is usually regarded as one of the highlights of a Chinese feast, and is at its best when it includes crab meat. It is also delicious when cooked with brown gravy from meat, duck or chicken prepared with soy sauce.

There are two forms of shark's fins selling in the market, the dried edible fins and that with the outer skin of the shark still covering the edible part. Fins with the outer skin on are more troublesome to prepare.

If you buy the fins still with the skin on, wash them and boil in enough water to cover them, for about 1 hour. Take them out and wash away the sand, fish meat and soft bones that may be still clinging to the fins. Put them back into clean water and boil again. Leave to cool until the water is lukewarm, again washing thoroughly. Repeat the process four or five times until you are left only with the edible part of the fins.

If you buy the dried edible part, only soak them in clean warm water for 12 hours before beginning to cook them. If desired they may be left soaking in the refrigerator for sometime until time for use. The weights given below are before soaking.

The fins should then be put in a bowl with enough chicken or meat stock to cover them and steamed over a medium fire 3 hours, or until they are soft. If you have no proper steamer, treat the bowl of fins as you would a steamed pudding by putting it in a couple of inches of water in a large pan. Make sure the water does not boil away, and keep the pan closely covered. Drain before using.

蟹 肉 魚 翅

Shark's Fins With Crab Meat

Meat of 2 carbs   2 eggs
1 t-sp salt   6 tb-sp lard
½ lb. skinless fins   2 slices ginger

Steam the crabs and take out the meat from the shell and the claws. Heat the lard and pour in the crab meat and beaten eggs. Stir fast for

Shark's Fins

1 minute add salt and ginger shreds. Mix in the already softened shark's fins and then remove from fire and serve.

紅 燒 魚 翅
Shark's Fins With Brown Sauce

½ lb. skinless fins ½ tb-sp cornflour
2 cups of brown gravy 2 tb-sp soy sauce

Warm the gravy and pour on the already softened shark's fins, cook for 10 minutes. Mix the cornflour with half a cup of water, add two tablespoonful of soy sauce and heat until boiling, then pour it into the dish.

魚 翅 湯
Shark's Fins Soup

½ lb. skinless fins ½ tb-sp salt
3 rice bowls of chicken soup 2 oz. ham (cooked)

Warm the chicken soup or meat soup. Add ½ tb-sp. salt. Pour in the already soften shark's fins and cook for 10 minutes. Sprinkle the minced ham on top of the soup before serving.

蝦 仁 魚 翅
Shark's Fins With Shrimps

½ lb. skinless fins 6 tb-sp soy sauce
½ lb. pork 6 tb-sp lard
½ lb. cabbage 4 slices ham
½ lb. shrimps 4 slices bamboo shoots
1 t-sp sugar 1 tb-sp cornflour
2 cups brown gravy ½ t-sp salt
4 tb-sp sherry (optional)

Wash the stalks of the cabbage and save the leaves for some other purpose. Cut vegetables into 2 inches section shreds. Heat 2 tb-sp lard till hot and fry the vegetables stalks for 3 minutes. Remove from pan. The pork selected should be tender. Cut the pork into shreds and shell

Shark's Fins

the shrimps. Cook the shrimps in a cup of water and ½ t-sp salt for 2 minutes after boiling. Heat 4 tb-sp oil and fry the meat shreds for 5 minutes, add in the sherry and soy sauce together with the cabbage stalks, and boil them on a medium fire for 10 minutes then add 2 cups of the brown gravy and keep on cooking for 10 minutes more. Pour on the already softened shark's fins and cook continuously for 2 or 3 minutes. Mix the cornflour in ½ cup of water and pour it into the pot with sugar. When it boils again place it on a big plate or bowl and arrange the sliced ham, 4 slices of bamboo shoots and shelled shrimps on top of the shark's fin. Serve hot.

Chop Suey

雜 碎 的 起 源

How *Chop Suey* Was First Created

One cannot write about Chinese food without making some references to the famous dish known in the West as *"Chop Suey,"* moreover, one should not only learn how to cook the dish but also know its historical origin.

"Chop Suey" is pronounced *"Tsa Siu"* in Mandarin, and it literally means mixed fragments. *"Chop Suey"* is served in most Chinese restaurants in the big cities of Europe and America. The reason for its popularity is that probably it has no strong flavour or taste of any kind and is, therefore, more easily acceptable to Western palates. It may also be due to the fact that it gives Westerners an idea of novelty and a kind of exotic experience although it is not a genuine Chinese dish, yet being quite distinct from Western food.

There are many legends about its origin. Here is the story most current in China. When the illustrious Chinese Ambassador Li Hung-Chang of the Ching Dynasty visited the United States he asked his servant to prepare him some Chinese food after he had been having foreign food for months. Unable to obtain the necessary Chinese vegetables, condiments, and other essentials, the servant did the best he could, and concocted a sort of hash which was destined to be the ancestor of *"Chop Suey."*

It matters little whether the story is true or not. Some say that it was a creation of a Chinese cook in a mining area in America, who, when asked to serve food at late hours of the night, used up the remnants of the pantry. Other say that it was first served in some Chinese coastal towns to foreign sailors at small food stalls. No matter what its origin may be, *"Chop Suey"* has always been a popular dish of the Western patrons of Chinese restaurants.

The following recipe shows how it is made.

Chop Suey

雜 碎

Chop Suey

(Basic Recipe)

½ lb. chicken	1 t-sp sugar
¼ lb. ham	¼ lb. cooking oil
½ lb. pork	1 tb-sp soy sauce
10 mushrooms	1 tb-sp cornflour
1 small bunch celery	1 t-sp salt
1 t-sp sherry (optional)	½ lb. bamboo shoots

Mince the pork and mix it well with ½ t-sp salt, cornflour and 2 tb-sp water. Soak the mushrooms in warm water for 10 minutes and cut all the other ingredients into small pieces, putting them on one side.

Take a saucepan, put in the oil and make it very hot. Use the hands to make the minced pork into small balls about the size of pigeon's eggs, and fry for 5 minutes; then remove from fire.

Leave about 4 tb-sp of oil in the pan to fry the chicken. Stir constantly for 1 minute.

Mix with the fried meat balls, pour in the sherry and soy sauce and cook for another 3 minutes. Take everything out and quickly rinse the pan then take four tablespoonfuls of oil, heat until smoking and add the mushrooms, sectioned celery, and sliced bamboo shoots. Stir for 1 minute and add ½ t-sp salt.

Pour in the cooked chicken, ham and meat balls and cook a further 3 minutes. A little water may be added if desired to obtain the right consistency.

蕃 茄 雜 碎

Tomato *Chop Suey*

Follow the basic recipe. Add two tomatoes, cut into 16 pieces to vegetables.

菠 蘿 雜 碎

Pineapple *Chop Suey*

Follow the basic recipe. Add 1 cup sliced pineapple to vegetables.

Chop Suey

青 椒 雜 碎

Green Pepper *Chop Suey*

Follow the basic recipe. Add 2 large sliced green pepper to vegetables.

雞 雜 雜 碎

Chicken Giblet *Chop Suey*

Use same method and ingredients as the basic recipe. Eliminate chicken meat. Use 3 sets of chicken giblets, slice very thin.

Note: One cup of green peas, broccoli sprouts, asparagus, or cabbage, may be added to any kind of *Chop Suey*. Other variations may be obtained by substituting for chicken, duck, mutton, beef, turkey, fish, lobster, crabmeat and shrimp. One cup of almonds, fungus, walnuts or white nuts may also be added.

雜　料

Seasonings

Since some of the Chinese seasonings are not available in Western markets or some say that they have great trouble in obtaining them, some ways of making the most common seasonings are given below.

黑　醬　油

Dark Soy Bean Sauce

10 lbs. soy beans	10 lbs. flour
10 lbs. salt	4½ gallons water

Boil the water and place it in a large jar with the salt. It should then be left for four or five days before the fermented beans are added.

To ferment the beans bring them to the boil in just enough water to cover them. Remove from the fire, cover tightly and leave overnight. They should be stirred and the beans should not be allowed to coagulate into lumps.

Drain off the water and mix the beans with the flour, making sure the beans are quite cold. Spread them out and cover with a piece of cloth to prevent the air getting at the beans. After two days they should be dried in the sun for three or four days, when they can be added to the salted water.

Be sure the beans are well-fermented—when they are in the right condition they are yellow and hairy.

The jar with the brine and beans should be left in the open day and night, covering it only to keep out rain. The ingredients will gradually darken; the longer the mixture it left in the sun the darker it will become.

The mixture is ready to use after about five weeks.

It should be drained into a clean vessel and left in the sun a few days longer. The liquid from the top of the jar is the sauce and the thick refuse is the "soy jam."

Seasonings

If the sauce shows signs of continuing its fermentation it should be filtered, brought to the boil and then sealed in bottles.

白 醬 油
Light Soy Bean Sauce

10 cups soy beans   6 gallons water
½ cup salt

Mix all ingredients together and cook until boiling. Turn to a low fire and simmer 5 hours or until five gallons of water is left. Drain and pour in a 3 gallons jar. Seal airtight. Leave the whole jar in the sun, about 1 year or more. The liquid is light soy bean sauce. The beans could be used to make Soy Bean Jam.

蠔 油
Oyster Sauce

1 gallon fresh oysters   4 slices ginger
3 tb-sp salt   2 gallons water
4 cloves crushed garlic   2 cups light soy sauce
4 young leeks (white   2 tb-sp sugar
   portion only)   ½ cup cornflour

Put the fresh oysters, salt crushed garlic, ginger, young leeks and 2 gallons of water in a large pot. Heat until boiling. Turn to a low fire and simmer for 5 hours or until about 1 gallon of water is left. Mix the soy sauce, sugar and cornflour with 1½ cups of water; stir well and add to the oysters gradually. Simmer for another 20 minutes. Drain and pour the sauce in airtight bottle and keep in a cool place. Dry the oysters in the sun and keep for future use.

辣 椒 醬
Chinese Chili Sauce

½ lb. red pepper   2 tb-sp crushed garlic
⅓ lb. apricots   10 cups water
2 tb-sp preserved lemon

Grind the red pepper, apricots, preserved lemon and garlic. Cook in 10 cups of water until to a boil; then turn to a low fire and simmer continuously for 1½ hours. Pour in airtight jar and keep in a warm place or, if possible, facing the sun for 3 months or longer.

甜 醬
Sweet Soy Jam

4 lbs. horse bean	3 lbs. salt
4 lbs. flour	2 gallons water

Soak the beans over night. Shell and skin the beans. Put enough water in a boiler to cover the beans and boil on a medium fire until the beans are soft. Mix with flour and make into cakes. Put them back into the boiler and boil again for 10 minutes. Take them out and put them on a flat tray. Leave so for a week until the flour and beans are fermented. Dry them in the sunshine for two or three days At the same time that beans are being dried in the sun, mix the salt with the water in a jar and expose the whole jar in the sun for a few days before the fermented beans and flour are put in. Turn occasionally after the fermented beans are soaked. Cover the jar during rainy days but not during the night if there is no rain. In about a month the sweet soy jam will be ready for use.

黃 汁
Brown Gravy

4 cups water or soup	1 t-sp salt
1 t-sp cornflour	1 t-sp soy sauce

Heat the water or soup in a deep saucepan until boiling. Mix salt, soy sauce, cornflour with ¾ cup water and add into the soup. Cook until translucent and serve hot.

麻 油
Sesame Oil

1 lb sesame seed

Stir the sesame seeds in a hot, heavy iron pan on a low fire until brown. Remove from fire and put them in a big bowl. Rub with fingers to make them into a form of powder. Pour gradually the boiling water in the bowl and mix into a paste. Use a spoon to scoop off the oil on the top of the paste. One pound of sesame seeds will be able to make

Seasonings

3 to 9 oz. of sesame oil which is much cheaper than that sold in the market. It is quite handy to make the sesame oil at home in those countries where such oil is not available in the market.

醋

Vinegar

5 lbs sherry
1 cup glutinous rice
1 cup of glutins rice (cooked)

Wash and clean the jar and pour in the wine with the cooked glutinous rice. Use a piece of iron stick but burn it over a fire until red. Put it in the jar until it becomes black. Continue to do this three times a day. After a month the vinegar is made and it is as excellent as the Chekiang black vinegar which is considered the best in China.

冰 糖

Rock Sugar

5 lbs sugar
5 eggs

Mix the sugar with enough water to cover it up. Heat on a low fire and boil for 15 minutes. Break the eggs into it and skim the scum until it is absolutely pure. When it is about crytalized, pour into a jar and use pieces of bamboo or anything that can be used as partitions for each layer. Seal the jar. The rock sugar is formed in a few days.

蝦 米

Dried Shrimps

5 lbs shrimps
1 lb. sherry (optional)
1 lb. salt

Wash the shrimps. Boil enough water to cover the shrimps and mix in the salt. Add in the sherry and boil for 5 minutes after the water starts to boil. Remove from fire and drain. Take off the heads and put on a tray to dry in the sunshine. When thoroughly dried put them in a dry bottle and keep for use.

Dried shrimps are very commonly used in Chinese cooking. It might be handy to make and preserve some dried shrimps at home.

INDEX

雞 Chicken

	Page
Braised Chicken	18
Braised Chicken with Mushrooms	19
Braised Chicken with Chestnuts	19
White-Jellied Chicken	20
Paper-Wrapped Chicken	20
Water-Melon Chicken	21
Beggar's Chicken	21
Steamed Chicken Wings and Legs	22
Steamed Chicken	22
Smoked Chicken	22
White-Cut Chicken	23
Chinese Chicken Salad	23
Chicken Fillet with Omelet	24
Assorted Chicken Dices	24
Fried Chicken Balls with Oyster Sauce	25
Fried Chicken with Green Pepper	25
Fried Chicken with Young Leeks	26
Chicken Shreds with Bamboo Shoots	26
Fried Diced Chicken with Walnuts	27
Fried Chicken with Mushrooms	27
Fried Chicken Liver and Gizzard with Mushrooms	27
Deep-Oil Fried Chicken	28
Fried Spring Chicken	28
Fried Chicken Breast	29
Deep Fried Chicken Gizzard	29

鴨 Duck

Whole Brown-Braised Duck	31
Braised Duck with Chestnuts	32
Wine-Simmered Duck	32
Roast Duck	32
Fairy Duck	33
Nanking Salt-Water Duck	33
Eight-Precious Duck	34
Fried Stuffed-Duck with Glutinous Rice	35
Fried Duck Shreds with Ginger	35

魚 Fish   Page

Steamed Shad 39
Braised Shad 39
Steamed Fish Slices 40
Meat Stuffed Fish 40
Fried Salted Fish 40
Fried Fish with Mushrooms 41
Braised Carp 41
Deep Fried Fish 41
Braised Eel 42
Fried Eel 42
Braised Turtle 42
Steamed Turtle 43
Fish Balls 43
Steamed Fish (whole) 44

猪肉 Pork

Braised Pork Leg (whole) 47
Braised Pork (whole) 47
Braised Pork (pieces) 47
Braised Pork Chop 48
Braised Pork with Cabbage 48
Braised Pork with Pine-nuts 49
Braised Pork with Olive 49
Smoked Pork 50
Barbecued Pork 50
Roast Pork 50
Steamed Minced Pork 51
White-Cut Meat 51
Sweet and Salted Pork 51
Steamed Bacon 52
Steamed Ham 52
Steamed Minced Meat with Salted Fish 52
Steamed Pork in Rice 53
Steamed Pork with Rice Powder 53
Meat Stuffed Mushrooms 54
Fried Pork Cutlets in Batter 54
Glutinous Rice Pork Balls 54
Pork Meat Balls with Cabbage 55
Fried Bean Curd and Pork Balls 55
Fried Pork Balls 56

	Page
Braised Lion's Head	56
Fried Pork Shreds with Celery	57
Fried Pork Shreds with Bamboo Shoots	57
Fried Slices Pork with French Beans	58
Fried Pork Shreds with Pea Sprouts	58
Fried Pork Tenderloin	58
Braised Tripe with Glutinous Rice	59
Braised Tripe	59
Fried Kidney with Bamboo Shoots	60
Fried Kidney with Cauliflower	60
Fried Liver	61

牛肉 Beef

Braised Beef (whole)	62
Braised Beef (in pieces)	62
Braised Beef with Carrots and Potatoes	62
Braised Beef Tripe with Tomato and Onion	63
Braised Beef with Tomato and Onion	63
Braised Ox Tongue	64
Smoked Sliced Beef	64
Smoke Beef Balls	64
Beef Balls	65
Fried Beef Slices with Onion	65
Fried Beef with Green Pepper	66
Fried Beef Liver	66
Fried Beef Slices and Mushrooms	66
Fried Beef with Celery	67
Fried Beef in Oyster Sauce	67
Fried Beef with Tomato	68
Steamed Beef	68
Spiced Beef Shreds	68

羊肉 Mutton And Lamb

Braised Mutton or Lamb	69
Stewed Mutton with Orange Peel	70
Cold Jellied Lamb or Mutton	70
Fried Lamb with Onions	71
Fried Lamb with Young Leeks	71
Fried Lamb with Chinese Vermicelli	71
Fried Lamb Slices	72

野味 Game   Page

Fried Wild Duck 73
Braised Spiced Wild Duck 73
Salted Pheasant 74
Fried Pheasant 74
Braised Pigeon 74
Deep-Fried Spiced Pigeon 75
Fried Spiced Dove 75

海味 Sea Food

Crab Shreds 76
Steamed Eggs with Crab 77
Fried Crab Meat 77
Scallop with Eggs 77
Scallop Shreds 78
Fried Sea Slugs 78
Steamed Clams 78
Fried Abalone 79
Fried Squids 79
Oiled-Fried Sea Blubber 80
Sea Blubber Skin with Turnip Shreds 80
Fried- Lobsters Mushrooms 80
Deep Fried Lobster 81
Lobsters with Meat Sauce 81
Steamed Lobster 82
Fried Shelled Prawns with Bamboo Shoots 82
Fried Prawns with Shells 83
Drunken Shrimps 83
Oiled-Fried Prawns 84
Shrimps on Toast 84
Fried Shrimp Balls 84
Fried Prawns 85
Fried Prawns with Mushrooms 85
Fried Prawns with Green Peas 85
Prawn Fu-Yung 85
Phoenix-Tail Prawns 86

蛋 Egg

Egg Omelet with Meat Shreds 87
Scrambled Eggs with Shrimps 88
Steamed Ham and Egg 88
Fried Ham and Egg 88

	Page
Simmered Tripe with Eggs	89
Braised Pork and Eggs	89
Fried Ham Balls with Eggs	89
Egg Dumplings	90
Tea Eggs	90

菜 Vegetables

Chinese Radish Salad	92
Fried Spinach	93
Fried Mushrooms with Bean Curd	93
Fried Winter Melon	94
Fried Celery with Pea Sprout	94
Fried Celery	94
Fried Bean Sprouts	95
Braised Turnips	95
Turnip Tops	95
Fried Pea-Vines	96
Creamed Cabbage	96
Fried Long Beans	96
Fried String Beans with Bamboo Shoots	97
Steamed Eggplant	97
Dried Shrimps with Spinach	97
Fried Fresh Horse Beans	98
Fried Fresh Peas	98
Fried Lettuce	98
Fried Pumpkin	99
Fried Eggplant with Dried Shrimps	99
Fried Mushrooms	99
Fried Mushrooms with Bamboo Shoots	100
Creamed Bamboo Shoots	100

湯 Soup

Chicken Soup	103
White Fungis and Chicken Soup	103
Duck Soup	104
Steamed Beef Soup	104
Beef and Turnip Soup	104
Potato and Pork-Bone Soup	105
Pig's Lung Soup	105

Page

Pig's Brain Soup ...	105
Steamed Liver Soup	106
Pig's Trotter Soup	106
Pork-Bone or Chicken-Bone Soup	106
Mushrooms with Horse Bean Soup	107
Chicken Shreds and Mushroom Soup	107
Spinach and Pig's Liver Soup ...	107
Kidney Soup	108
Fish Soup ...	108
Fish Head and Turnip Soup	108
Meat Ball and Chinese Vermicelli Soup	109
Spinach Soup	109
Egg and Mushroom Soup ...	109
Steam Mushroom Soup	110
Mushroom and Bean Curd Soup	110
Cabbage and Bean Curd Soup ...	110
Thick Soup	111
Watercress Soup	111

中國火鍋 Chinese Chafing Dishes

Ten Variety Chafing Dish	112
Chrysanthemum Fish Chafing Dish	115

沙鍋 Sandy Pots

Sandy Pot Fish Head	116
Sandy Pot Bean Curd	116

飯 Rice

Boiled Rice	118
Steamed Rice	118
Cabbage and Ham Rice ...	119
Assorted Fried Rice	119
Egg and Rice	120
Fried Ham and Egg Rice	120
White Congee	120
Chicken Congee	121
Buddha Congee	121
Shrimp Congee	121

麵 Noodles

Fresh Noodles	124
Fried Vegetarian Noodles	124

	Page
Fried Noodles	125
Stewed Noodles	125
Fried Crispy Noodles	126
Chicken Soup Noodles	126
Soy Jam Noodles	127

麵食 Pastry

Steamed Bread or Man-T'ou	128
Steamed Stuffed Bread or Pao-Tzu	129
Rambling or Hun-T'un	130
Meat Dumpling or Chiao-Tzu	131
Patties	132
Spring Rolls	133
Fried Spring Onion Cake	135
Steamed Fancy Rolls	135

點心 Sweet Dishes

White Fungis Soup	136
Soy Bean Milk	136
Fried Pumpkin Balls	136
Fried Sweet Potatoes	137
Lotus Seed and Glutinous Rice Congee	137
Eight Precious Rice	138

糖醋類 Sweet And Sour Dishes

Sweet and Sour Sauce	139
Sweet and Sour Pork	140
Sweet and Sour Pork with Lichee	140
Sweet and Sour Pork Balls	140
Sweet and Sour Fish Balls	141
Sweet and Sour Lobster	141
Sweet and Sour Lobster with Pineapple	142
Sweet and Sour Lobster with Lichee	142
Sweet and Sour Clams	142
Sweet and Sour Fish	142
Sweet and Sour Shrimp	143
Sweet and Sour Shrimp Balls	143
Sweet and Sour Chicken	143
Sweet and Sour Chicken Balls	143
Sweet and Sour Scallops	144
Sweet and Sour Fresh Squid	144

Page

Sweet and Sour Eel	144
Sweet and Sour 100 Year Old Egg	145
Sweet and Sour Conch	145
Sweet and Sour Conch with Pineapple	146
Sweet and Sour Fish Slices	146
Sweet and Sour Ribs	147
Sweet and Sour Cabbage	147
Sweet and Sour Carrots	147
Sweet and Sour Mustard Green	148

燕窩 Bird's Nest

Birds' Nests with Minced Chicken	149
Birds' Nests with Cream Soup	150
Birds' Nests with Almond Soup	150
Pigeon Eggs and Birds' Nests Soup	150

魚翅 Shark's Fins

Shark's Fins with Crab Meat	151
Shark's Fins with Brown Sauce	152
Shark's Fins Soup	152
Shark's Fins with Shrimps	152

雜碎 Chop Suey

Tomato Chop Suey	155
Pineapple Chop Suey	155
Green Pepper Chop Suey	156
Chicken Giblet Chop Suey	156

雜料 Seasonings

Dark Soy Bean Sauce	157
Light Soy Bean Sauce	158
Oyster Sauce	158
Chinese Chili Sauce	158
Sweet Soy Jam	159
Brown Gravy	159
Sesame Oil	159
Vinegar	160
Rock Sugar	160
Dried Shrimps	160

THOMAS COWAN & CO., LTD.

White Ant & Pest Experts
Telephone 20281

WILL EXTERMINATE ALL THOSE HOUSEHOLD PESTS

White Ants and other *Termites*

Cockroaches and *Silverfish*

Rats and *Mice*

Dog Ticks

Hornets Bees

and

Borer Beetles

Makers of COWANS LIZARD Insect Spray

(The strongest Insecticide on the market.)

SECRETARIES

The **BORNEO** *Company Limited*
(INCORPORATED IN ENGLAND)

CROSBY HOUSE
SINGAPORE

MEMBER — INDUSTRIAL PEST CONTROL ASSOCIATION — IPCA — OF GREAT BRITAIN

KUALA LUMPUR — IPOH — MALACCA — PENANG

The PAVILION RESTAURANT

in

Orchard Road

can offer you

everything you would expect in

THE PIG

&

WHISTLE

in your own home town
(EXCEPT THE BUXOM BARMAID)

The "IDEAL MILK" for all CULINARY PURPOSES

"IDEAL" MILK, which is full-cream Unsweetened Condensed Milk, is obtainable from all Grocers. Always ask for "IDEAL" by name and not "Unsweetened" Milk, and you are sure of success with any of the recipes which call for milk.

Id.1/54

Australia's Finest ROLLER WHEAT FLOUR

Exporters:—
DODSON TRADING,
422, Collins Street,
Melbourne, Australia.

Trade enquiries to:—
TAN SEE TEE
23, Bonham Bldg.,
Singapore 1. Phone 6097.

Vanity

A dress for every occasion.

Chrisp   Kitchen   Frocks
Smart   Afternoon   Dresses
Elegant   Cocktail   Ensambles
Glamorous   Evening   Gowns

Hats — Gloves — Handbags — Flowers — Jewellery

For Product Safety Concerns and Information please contact our EU
representative GPSR@taylorandfrancis.com
Taylor & Francis Verlag GmbH, Kaufingerstraße 24, 80331 München, Germany

www.ingramcontent.com/pod-product-compliance
Lightning Source LLC
Chambersburg PA
CBHW061837300426
44115CB00013B/2417